P9-BIO-681

AFFRONTS, INSULTS AND INDIGNITIES

by
Morris Mandel

JONATHAN DAVID PUBLISHERS
MIDDLE VILLAGE, N. Y. 11379

AFFRONTS, INSULTS AND INDIGNITIES

by

Morris Mandel

JONATHAN DAVID PUBLISHERS
68-22 Eliot Avenue
Middle Village, N. Y. 11379

Library of Congress Cataloging in Publication Data

Mandel, Morris, 1911- comp.
Affronts, insults and indignities.

1. Invective. I. Title.
PN6231.I65M3 808.88'2 74-6568
ISBN 0-8246-0180-6

Printed in United States of America

TABLE OF CONTENTS

TO THE READER:
A Bit of Advice . . .

The aim of this provocative book is to arm every person with appropriate words, crowning jokes, cynical gags, pertinent anecdotes, artful barbs, and subtle roasts; for when you meet in verbal combat with your doctor, lawyer, tax collector, or butcher, baker, and candle-stick maker—not to mention your mate, employer, and next-door neighbor—you'd best be prepared.

In addition, when the opportunity arises for you to say a "few words," or act as M.C., this volume will help you demonstrate your sparkling wit by sprinkling your comments with humorous gags about life, politics, and the love of man for dogs, pets, and assorted bees, bugs and butterflies. You may very well end up the oratorical wit of the evening. All that is required is that you be adequately prepared with a selection of so-called adlibs to be found in abundance in these pages. If you doubt this, ask the experts: Bob Hope, Groucho Marx, Joey Adams, George Jessel, Don Rickles, and many, many others. Run for cover when they give you their studied replies.

It wasn't a simple matter to collect these animated, brilliant gems. The attempts to assemble this broad, diversified collection of affronts, insults and indignities led me to seek them out in the strangest places. I found them in the words of poets, on the lips of cabinet officers, in the writings of heads of state, in the ad-libs of comedians, in the speeches of politicians, and in the everyday conversation between husband and wife. I discovered them in the thousands of letters from people who share their problems with me. And, at times, I saw them inscribed for posterity on the forsaken walls of public bathrooms and subway stations. The source of the material is given whenever I have been able to verify its origin.

Let's spend a moment analyzing the definition of an insult. An insult is an instant retort, a sarcastic comeback, a punchy wise-crack, a devastating gag.

Wits of all ages have used the peppery insult to stop a person cold. What can be more effective in bringing people's frailties and foolishness into focus than a sharp, well-aimed, skillfully delivered barb? What better method has been devised to demolish a bore, boor, chiseler, nag, egotist, screwball, ass, stuffed shirt or gossip than a verbal brickbat? If, as Heywood

Broun, said, "Repartee is what you wish you'd said," then the preparatory course can be found within the pages of this book.

Repartee is perfect when it achieves its purpose, attacking with a double edge; it is a duel fought with jokes as sabres; it is intellect on the offensive. It calls a spade a spade with deadly accuracy and without the necessity of using a brickbat.

Insults can be divided into the everyday garden variety, and the more sophisticated type saved for hallowed halls. Telling a person "You're nothing but a half wit," is not nearly as effective as "Who saith you have an open mind; you just have nothing but holes in your head."

Always remember:

> Three things must insults, like bees, have all,
> A sting, and honey, and a body small.

Of course, caution must be used when it comes to affronts. Discretion must be applied, and it is wise for people who live in glass houses to refrain from playing with rocks. After all, an affront is a sharp tool to be handled with care, and not to be used by fools and children unless, that is, conversational suicide is contemplated.

And indignities—well that's most difficult to define. They fall somewhere between an insult and an affront. You will surely recognize it when you hear it or read it.

You can use this book best by allowing it to supercharge your conversation, speech and writings. Let its words serve as a spear, as your final thrust in an argument; it is your verbal knock-out blow. The conversational adversary whom you defeat with a good insult, affront or indignity will never rise again.

Here they are, then, several thousand of them, breezy one-liners and lengthier pieces: laconic missiles, tongue-whipping bristles, poetic jabs, and witty arrows, a veritable arsenal of satirical sallies.

Use them to advantage!

MORRIS MANDEL

September 1974

THE HUMAN RACE
Introduction

In a recently published book, the British zoologist Desmond Morris portrayed man as a "naked ape." Other scientists, both past and present, keep insisting that man evolved from the animal kingdom, though no animal has thus far presented himself to defend his ancestry . Referring to man as an ape is serious business, and it bogs us down in a welter of statements, opinions, arguments, and scientific surveys.

Countless groups come forward to rebel, to find fault. Among these are religionists, philosophers, psychologists, psychiatrists, anthropologists, curators of zoos—to name but a few. Alexander Graham Bell said: "man is an animal which alone among the animals refuses to be satisfied by the fulfillment of animal desires." "But man, never halting in his senseless career," continues Nicolas Boileau-Despreaux, "flits ceaselessly from thought to thought; his heart always at sea, amidst a thousand embarrassments, knows neither what it wishes, nor what it does not wish. What it one day detests, the next day it desires."

What indignities are heaped on man! Listen!

"Half dust, half deity, alike unfit to sink or soar."—Lord Byron.

"There are times when one would like to hang the whole human race, and finish the farce."—Mark Twain.

"When man is a brute, he is the most sensual and loathsome of all brutes."—Nathaniel Hawthorne.

Why all these insults? Why the comment of W. S. Gilbert?

Darwinian Man, though well-behaved,
At best is only a monkey shaved!

God made man a little lower than the angels, and there is much good that man has accomplished. Mark Twain disagrees and says, "Yes, God made man a little lower than the angels, and he has been getting a little lower ever since."

Twain, not completely satisfied with this left hook, wrote: "All that I care to know is that a man is a human being—that is enough for me; he can't be any worse."

I don't believe that man is but another animal species. If he is, why has no other species produced even one Darwin?

Man is a complex being, and each person has his own insanity. He has two eyes, two ears, and one mouth, yet, he speaks twice as much as he sees and hears. He is not like any other single creature; but he is like all of them collectively. He is sort of half-and-half—right in the middle, not close to being wise, and not far from being foolish. He is a world in miniature, a miracle.

Man has eyes with which to see the entire world, but cannot see his own faults. In the morning, he says "I wish it were evening." In the evening he says, "I wish it was morning." He always wants what he doesn't have, and wants to be where he isn't.

Diogenes carried not only a lantern with which he was in search of man, but, in case he should find one, he carried also a cudgel. Man can be very wise, and he can be as blundering as a bear. He is half angel and half brute.

A writer once observed: "Man embodies within himself all sorts of creatures: the cat playing with a mouse; the weasel stealing into a coop and turning the heads of the fowl; monkeys aping others; dogs wagging their tails for anyone who throws them a bone; a spider luring a fly, entangling it in its web, and sucking out its vitals; etc. . ."

But in reality what is this world without man? Truthfully, man is the world, despite his frailties, frustrations and failures. The following pages tell about man—what man thinks of man. It's all in fun so continue with your reading!

THE HUMAN RACE

If a man makes a stupid mistake, men say: "What a fool that man is." But if a woman makes a stupid mistake, men say, "What fools women are."

—Lowell Nussbaum

o o o

There are three kinds of lies: lies, damned lies, and statistics.

—Benjamin Disraeli

o o o

The more I see of mankind, the more I like my dog.

o o o

The world is divided into two classes: invalids and nurses.

—Whistler

o o o

If my theory of relativity is proven successful, Germany will claim me as German and France will declare that I am a citizen of the world. If my theory should prove to be untrue, then France will say that I am a German, and Germany will say that I am a Jew.

—Albert Einstein (1879-1955)

o o o

An expert is one who knows more and more about less and less.

—Nicholas Murray Butler

o o o

An expert is a person who avoids the small errors as he sweeps on to the grand fallacy.

—Benjamin Stolberg

o o o

"TO WHOM IT MAY CONCERN: Mr. Jack Lanning has worked for me for 25 years and when he left, I was perfectly satisfied."

o o o

He has a finger in every pot and a hand in nothing.

o o o

He promises too much too soon, and accomplishes too little, too late.

o o o

He walks unembarrassed, with nothing on his mind.

o o o

The reason he is so easily rattled is because he has a screw loose somewhere.

o o o

His narrow mind goes together with his broad tongue.

o o o

They never taste who always drink;
They always talk who never think.

—Matthew Prior

o o o

He has one pair of eyes, yet draws dry a hundred tongues.

o o o

They can be meek that have no other cause.

—Shakespeare, *Richard III*

o o o

Fish and guests smell at three days old.

o o o

Here lies one whose name was writ in water.

—Keats, *Epitaph*

o o o

If living is an art, then most people's lives resemble more doodling than art.

o o o

He has nothing to say but you have to listen long to find it out.

o o o

His head is like a door-knob; anyone can turn it.

o o o

The public be damned.

—Vanderbilt

o o o

Brainless mastery feeds on spineless followers.

o o o

He is a "smart alec" who makes faces at what he cannot face up to.

o o o

The reason why it is so hard for him to get new ideas in his head is because they can't squeeze in between his prejudices.

o o o

He doesn't have a clear conscience, just a poor memory.

o o o

Many a strong back hides a weak backbone.

o o o

He thinks he is headstrong when, in truth, he is brain-weak.

o o o

His mind seems to have suffered from infantile paralysis.

o o o

Most people who have nothing on their minds have nothing in them.

o o o

He works like a horse so everybody rides him.

o o o

Don't worry about finding your proper place in life; somebody is sure to tell you.

o o o

A wise guy stopped a street bus the other morning and said to the driver, "Well, Noah, you got here at last. Is the ark full?"

"Not quite," replied the driver. "We need one more monkey, so come aboard."

o o o

As a rule a man's a fool;
When it's hot he wants it cool;
When it's cool he wants it hot.
Always wanting what is not.

o o o

Someone has said that the world's greatest area of underdeveloped territory lies under people's hats.

o o o

Mark Twain, checking in at a hotel in Canada, noticed that the arrival just ahead of him had written on the hotel register, "Baron von Blank and valet." Mark Twain was not to be outdone by this show of elegance. He wrote: "Mark Twain and valise."

o o o

When the Nazis urged the King of Denmark to institute anti-Jewish legislation, he replied, "But you see, there isn't any Jewish problem here. We do not consider ourselves inferior to them."

o o o

People are funny. They spend money they don't have, to buy things they don't need, to impress folks they don't like.

o o o

A gossip can be compared to a broom which can sweep the whole place clean but itself remains dirty.

o o o

The brain is like a freight car—guaranteed to have a certain capacity, but often running empty.

o o o

When a young man asked a young lady, "I don't know what to do with my week-end?" she answered: "Why not put your hat on it?"

o o o

The sign read: "SCHOOL-DON'T KILL A CHILD." Beneath was a childish scrawl: "WAIT FOR A TEACHER."

o o o

Admetus: "How do you like this extraordinary epitaph that I've written for myself?"

Demonax: "It's so beautiful, I wish it were in place already."

o o o

Some people think they have a dynamic personality because they are always exploding.

o o o

You may be puffed up with conceit but that hardly makes you a swell guy.

o o o

He has a chip on his shoulder which is a positive sign of wood higher up.

o o o

He may be burning with enthusiasm, but that doesn't mean

he's so hot.

° ° °

Some people drink deeply at the fountain of knowledge—others just gargle.

° ° °

My uncle calls fishing, a jerk at one end of the line waiting for a jerk at the other end.

° ° °

He tried his hand at something new and failed; next time he ought to try his head.

° ° °

Many wise words are spoken in jest, but they don't compare with the number of foolish words spoken in earnest.

° ° °

He is too fond of people who agree with him and food that doesn't.

° ° °

Most folks who slap us on the back expect us to cough up something.

° ° °

He doesn't have to be in the rain to be all wet.

° ° °

His open mind should be closed for repairs.

° ° °

If he ever sold hats, people would be born without heads.

° ° °

Many people who stand on their dignity have precious little standing room.

° ° °

Some owe success in life to luck
Some owe it to their mothers;
But most acclaim the good advice
They didn't take from others.

—*Sunshine Magazine*

° ° °

It is a pity that he is thoughtless rather than speechless.

° ° °

We know a guy who isn't exactly overpaid, but they should gift-wrap his pay check.

° ° °

Since Nature abhors a vacuum, she usually fills an empty head with conceit.

° ° °

He thinks he's cooking on the front burner, but in truth he's only half-baked.

o o o

Here's a fact that's worth the knowing,
So treasure and mark it well;
When the mind is through with growing
Then the head begins to swell.

—*Sunshine Magazine*

o o o

If he could see himself as others see him, he would never take a second look.

o o o

If you get up earlier in the morning than your neighbor, and work harder and scheme more and stick closer to your job, and stay up later planning how to make more money than your neighbor, and burn the midnight oil planning how to get ahead of him while he's snoozing, not only will you leave more money when you die than he will, but you will leave it much sooner.

o o o

The only way he thinks he can have a good time is by making a fool of himself.

o o o

The trouble with our American "melting pot" is that all the scum rises to the top.

o o o

If we wish to make a new world, we have the materials ready. The first one was made out of chaos.

o o o

If ignorance is bliss, why isn't he the happiest man in the world?

o o o

If "what you don't know can't hurt you" is true, then he's absolutely "hurtproof."

o o o

He pours anti-knock into his car when he should be taking it himself.

o o o

He thinks he is carrying the world on his shoulders when the only thing he's carrying is a swelled head.

o o o

He avoids criticism by saying nothing, doing nothing, and being nothing.

° ° °

It is man who claims kinship with the apes; no ape has yet acknowledged it.

° ° °

A committee is a group of the unwilling, chosen by the uninformed, to accomplish the impossible.

° ° °

A conference is a collection of important people who singly can do nothing, but when they meet together can decide that nothing can be done.

° ° °

The donkey may hide his ears, but his voice will betray him.

—Russian proverb

° ° °

Eggs want to be smarter than hens.

° ° °

A cat and a rat will make peace over a carcass.

° ° °

When asked why he had resigned from the Friars Club, Groucho Marx answered: "I don't want to belong to any club that would accept me as one of its members."

° ° °

When he was approached at a party by a man who inquired, "Remember me, Groucho?" the funny man answered, "I never forget a face, but in your case I'll make an exception."

° ° °

Dorothy Parker, who was bored at a weekend party, sent the following telegram to a friend: "Please send me a loaf of bread—and enclose a saw and file."

° ° °

"No, son, you can't wear your hair like Elvis Presley."
"Why not? You wear yours like Yul Brynner."

° ° °

He's a real magician; he always makes an ass out of himself.

° ° °

You can write about his accomplishments on a piece of confetti.

° ° °

There's a bus leaving in five minutes; he ought to get under it.

° ° °

That's not a chip on his shoulder; that's his head.

° ° °

A celebrity is somebody who is known by many people he's glad he doesn't know.

∘ ∘ ∘

He's very cultured—he can bore you on any subject.

∘ ∘ ∘

His greatest work of fiction was filling out his income tax return.

∘ ∘ ∘

"I've had a wonderful evening," said Groucho Marx to his hostess as he was leaving a dull party, "but this wasn't it."

∘ ∘ ∘

A committee is a group of the unfit, appointed by the unwilling to do the unnecessary.

—Victor Riesel

∘ ∘ ∘

The mob has many heads, but no brains.

—Thomas Fuller

∘ ∘ ∘

Epitaph: A statement that usually lies above about the one who lies below.

∘ ∘ ∘

Every hero becomes a bore at last.

—Ralph Waldo Emerson

∘ ∘ ∘

William Lloyd Garrison is a tart Luther who neighs like a horse.

—Ibid

∘ ∘ ∘

Imagination: A warehouse of facts, with poet and liar in joint ownership.

—Ambrose Bierce

∘ ∘ ∘

He is like an automobile; the less substantial he becomes, the more knocking he does.

∘ ∘ ∘

He is so conceited that I'd like to buy him at my price and sell him at his.

∘ ∘ ∘

He is so wrapped up in himself that he makes a small package.

∘ ∘ ∘

Education might broaden his mind but what can be done for

his big head?

o o o

They made a fool out of him because he had the right material for the job.

o o o

He constantly loses his head and is the last one to miss it.

o o o

He is so stupid that he walked into an antique shop and asked, "What's new?"

o o o

He is so stupid, he walked into a crematorium and asked, "What's cooking?"

o o o

Mark Twain said that April 1 is the day upon which we are reminded of what we are on the other 364.

o o o

"Don't be so nervous," whispered the fight manager. "Remember, if he was any good he wouldn't be fighting you."

o o o

He is the type of genius who can do anything except make a living.

o o o

I am free of all prejudice. I hate everyone equally.

—W. C. Fields

o o o

For the Jews I am a Christian, for the Christians a Jew, for the Russians a German, for the Germans a Russian, for the classicists a futurist, for the futurists a retrograde. From this I conclude that I am neither fish nor meat—a sorrowful individual indeed.

—Anton Rubinstein (1830-1894)

o o o

Cemetery: An isolated suburban spot where mourners match lies, poets write at a target and stone-cutters spell for a wager.

—Ibid

o o o

A man with your low intelligence should have a voice to match.

—Lord Mancroft (to a heckler with a loud voice)

o o o

He works like a horse and everyone rides him.

o o o

He wouldn't be a fool if he did not possess such suitable material for the job.

o o o

Unfortunately he has nothing to say, but cannot be persuaded not to say it.

° ° °

He is the kind of a bore, who when you ask him how he feels, he tells you.

° ° °

A bore is a fellow who opens his mouth and puts his feats in it.

—Henry Ford

° ° °

He can compress the fewest ideas in the most words of any man I ever met.

—Abraham Lincoln (referring to a famous windbag)

° ° °

If you have her for a friend you don't need enemies.

—June Allyson

° ° °

He finds faults as if it were a buried treasure.

—F. O. Walsh

° ° °

Highly educated bores are by far the worst; they know so much, in such fiendish detail, to be boring about.

—Louis Kronenberger

° ° °

In Balaam's time it was considered a miracle when an ass spoke. Now we think nothing of it when they drive cars.

° ° °

Some people are like French bread—little dough, but lots of crust.

° ° °

Little men who want to be remembered start great wars.

° ° °

The trouble with him was that when he got to greener pastures, he couldn't climb the fence.

° ° °

He is one of the world's great fault-finders, and he keeps whatever he finds.

° ° °

What trouble he goes to. He became a Lion, an Elk, and an Eagle—just to prove he's not a skunk.

° ° °

He thinks he is a self-starter when all he is is only a crank.

° ° °

The trouble with self-made men is that they quit the job too early.

° ° °

He thinks he is presidential timber but he's only another splinter.

° ° °

The sewing-circle—the Protestant confessional, where each one confesses, not her own sins, but the sins of her neighbors.

—Charles B. Fairbanks (1827-1859)

° ° °

If a little knowledge is dangerous, then he is in great peril.

° ° °

Some folks have the presence of mind and the absence of thought.

° ° °

Some men chisel out a career, he just chisels.

° ° °

Some young fellows would make a bigger success of things if they had a little more horsepower and less exhaust.

° ° °

There are two valid reasons why some people don't mind their own business—they haven't any mind and they haven't any business.

° ° °

The brain is a wonderful organ. It starts working the moment you get up in the morning, and does not stop until you get to the office and start dictating.

° ° °

Any fool can criticise, condemn, and complain—and most of them do.

—Dale Carnegie

° ° °

"If there are any dumbbells in the room, please stand up."

After a long pause a lone freshman stood up in the rear.

"Why do you consider yourself a dumbbell?" asked the professor.

"I don't," was the answer, "but I hate to see you standing all alone."

° ° °

Douglas Jerrold, a 19th century wit, was one day approached by a chatty bore. "Well, what's going on?" asked the bore of Jerrold.

The reply came swiftly, "I am," and he did.

° ° °

Oliver Wendell Holmes, having been at an afternoon tea, authoritatively defined such functions for all times as: Giggle, Gabble, Gobble, Git!

° ° °

He is such an egotist that at a wedding he wants to be the bridegroom, and at a funeral, he wants to be the corpse.

° ° °

"I have a previous engagement which I will make as soon as possible," said John Barrymore, turning down an invitation from a bore.

° ° °

The fellow who said, "What's the use," is not the locomotive —he's only the caboose.

° ° °

Turning to a talkative lady sitting at his side, Samuel Johnson said, "Madam, I'm very fond of the company of ladies; I like their beauty, I like their delicacy, I like their vivacity, and I like their silence."

° ° °

I overheard my mother passing along to my father a newsy tidbit concerning a neighbor. "You know you shouldn't repeat stories about others," I said with mock seriousness. "That makes you a gossip."

"I'm not a gossip!" she snapped back. "I'm a news analyst."

—James I. Savage, *Reader's Digest*

° ° °

I never make a move without first ignoring my press agent.

—Groucho Marx

° ° °

In Hollywood, a starlet is the name for any woman under thirty who is not actively employed in a brothel.

—Ben Hecht

° ° °

A clerk was handed a pay envelope which, through error, contained a blank check. The astonished clerk looked at it and moaned: "Just what I knew would happen eventually. They're paying me what I'm worth."

° ° °

He won't leave any footprints on the sands of time because he is too busy covering his tracks.

° ° °

He hasn't stored up enough treasure in heaven to make the down payment on a harp.

° ° °

He sticks with his friends until debt do them part.

—Bob Goddard, *St. Louis Globe-Democrat*

° ° °

George, looking at Niagara Falls: "Got anything like that in Texas?"

Texan: "We got a plumber who could fix that leak in ten minutes."

° ° °

When she gives you a piece of her mind it's always a long and narrow one.

—*Washington Iowa Journal*

° ° °

He has the ability to speak in several languages, but unfortunately does not have the ability to stop in any of them.

° ° °

Lives of ancestors remind us,
We give photos to our kin; and,
Departing, leave behind us relatives
Who point and grin.

° ° °

He's the kind of guy who would like to die in his own arms.

—Buzzie Bavasi

° ° °

When a man runs for Congress, you are a friend; when he is elected, you are a constituent; and when he's in office you are just a taxpayer.

—Lou Erickson, *Atlanta Journal*

° ° °

A specialist is a person who knows very much about very little and continues to learn more and more about less and less until eventually he knows practically everything about almost nothing at all.

° ° °

Someone once gave this definition of a jury: twelve men with average ignorance.

° ° °

If a cluttered desk indicates a cluttered mind, what does my husband's empty desk indicate?

° ° °

If criticism had any real power to harm, the skunk would be

extinct by now.

° ° °

There's a new and expensive perfume called "Evening in Arabia"—it smells just like gasoline.

—Tiger Lyons, quoted by Robert J. Herguth

° ° °

A gossip is one who suffers from acute indiscretion.

° ° °

People, like boats, toot loudest when in a fog.

° ° °

When a man starts throwing dirt, you can be sure he's losing ground.

° ° °

He walks as if balancing the family tree on his nose.

—Raymond Moley

° ° °

Dear Sirs,

Some day you will move me almost to the verge of irritation by your chuckle-headed goddamned fashion of shutting your goddamned gas off without giving any notice to your goddamned parishioners. Several times you have come within an ace of smothering half of this household in their beds and blowing up the other half by this idiotic, not to say criminal, cut of yours. And it has happened again today. Haven't you a telephone?

—S.L. Clemens

(Letter sent by Mark Twain to Hartford Gas Company on Feb. 12, 1891—*Mark Twain's Notebook*, edited by Albert Bigelow Paine, Harper & Row)

° ° °

George Bernard Shaw was a noted vegetarian. At a dinner with Sir James Barrie, Shaw was once served a vegetarian concoction. Barrie looked at Shaw's plate and remarked, "Tell me, my good friend, have you eaten or are you going to?"

° ° °

Letter from a debtor to the bank who had threatened legal action:

If you ain't better prepared to meet your God than I am to meet this obligation, you shore are going to hell.

° ° °

The trouble with TV dinners is that a man has to listen to his wife's commercial as to why she's serving them.

—Dan Bennett

° ° °

It's true of all our house guests,
I've learned it to my sorrow.
Although they may be here today,
They're seldom gone tomorrow.

° ° °

Don't worry if your "you" is small and
your rewards are few:
Remember that the mighty oak
was once a nut like you.

° ° °

"He says he's related to you, and can prove it."
"The man's a fool."
"That may be just coincidence."

° ° °

Some careers are carved; his is chiseled.

° ° °

The mouth is the grocer's friend, the dentist's fortune, the orator's pride, and the fool's trap.

° ° °

"Opened by mistake" applies more often to open mouths than it does to mail.

° ° °

Use your head; it's the little things that count.

° ° °

He got two orders on his first day as a salesman: GET OUT and STAY OUT!

° ° °

You can always get someone to love you—even if you have to do it yourself.

—Tom Masson

° ° °

Among the footprints in the sands of time some people leave only the marks of a heel.

° ° °

Don't be obnoxious—leave that to me.

° ° °

He may look busy, but he's only confused.

° ° °

It isn't necessary to be a half-wit to work here, but it helps a lot.

° ° °

Work fascinates him. He can sit and look at it for hours.

° ° °

He opens nothing more by mistake than his mouth.

o o o

Usually the biggest nut is not to be found on the wheel, but behind it.

o o o

The emptier the head, the less it takes to fill it.

o o o

A wise man thinks all he says; a fool says all he thinks.

o o o

The trouble with most open minds is that they are open at both ends.

o o o

Most of his trouble is caused by too much bone in the head and not enough in the back.

o o o

Don't punch a man in the nose when he calls you a fool. Just quietly take an inventory—he may be right.

o o o

The first screw that got loose in his head is the one that controlled his tongue.

o o o

Let the meek inherit the earth—they have it coming to them.

—James Thurber

o o o

The man who constantly stands on his dignity is located on a mighty slippery spot.

o o o

There are times when, if you are not feeling like yourself, it is quite an improvement.

o o o

"Now, if you have that in your head," said a professor who had just explained a theory to his students, "it's all in a nutshell."

o o o

He is like a sponge. He sops up a great deal, and unless someone presses hard, he yields nothing.

o o o

When I consider how we fret
About a woman or a debt,
And strive and strain and carp and cuss
And work and want and sweat and fuss,
And then observe the monkey swing
A casual tail at everything,

I am inclined to think that he
Evolved from apes like you and me.

—Samuel Hoffenstein (1890-1947)

o o o

He not only overflowed with learning, but stood in the slop.

—Rev. Sydney Smith

o o o

The path of civilization is paved with tin cans.

—Elbert Hubbard

o o o

I have great faith in fools. Self-confidence, my friends call it.

—Edgar Allan Poe

o o o

There is nothing so stupid as an educated man, if you get him off the things he was educated in.

—Will Rogers

o o o

The pious ones of Plymouth, reaching the Rock, first fell upon their knees, and then upon the Aborigines.

—William Evarts

o o o

Life is just one damned thing after another.

—Frank Ward O'Malley

o o o

It is not true that life is one damn thing after another; it's one damn thing over and over.

—Edna St. Vincent Millay

o o o

Our whole civilization is based on a hypothetical future and the idiocy of fortune tellers.

—Stephen Vizinczey

o o o

Life is a banquet and most poor sons of bitches are starving to death.

o o o

—Patrick Dennis

o o o

The best way to convince a fool that he is wrong is to let him have his own way.

—Josh Billings

o o o

A radical is a guy who can out-talk you on any subject.

o o o

His clear conscience is a result of a poor memory.

° ° °

Great minds discuss ideas; average minds discuss events; very small minds discuss people.

° ° °

The average man has 66 pounds of muscle and 3.3 pounds of brain, according to a physician. Maybe that explains a lot of things.

° ° °

Noisy diner in an elegant hotel dining room: "What do you have to do to get a glass of water in this dump?"

Manager: "Why don't you try setting yourself on fire!"

° ° °

He's got to be little to belittle.

° ° °

She is descended from a long line that her mother listened to.

—Gypsy Rose Lee

° ° °

No person ever knew so much that was so little to the purpose.

—Ralph Waldo Emerson

° ° °

When a famous rabbi, on a certain holiday was sent a picture of a pig as a present, he sent back a photograph of himself, with the words, "You sent me a picture of yourself, I send you mine."

° ° °

The world of fools has such a store
 That he who would not see an ass
Must hide at home, and bolt his door,
 And break his looking-glass.

—La Monnays

° ° °

Young men think old men are fools;
But old men know young men are fools.

—George Chapman

° ° °

Four thousand people cross London Bridge every day, mostly fools.

—T. Carlyle

° ° °

The emptier the pot, the quicker it boils—he ought to watch his temper.

° ° °

He's so fat because he lives from hand to mouth.

° ° °

He did me as many good turns as a cork-screw.

—Brendan Behan

° ° °

He was as tight as a drum and so made the most noise.

° ° °

Upper-crust is a bunch of crumbs held together by their own dough.

° ° °

It is almost impossible for you to be as ignorant as your employees think you are.

° ° °

He ought to blow his brains out; he's got nothing to lose.

° ° °

He has one natural tendency—being obnoxious.

° ° °

He is the type of man who keeps on making mountains out of molehills by adding a little dirt.

° ° °

When he talks about others, he is a gossip. And when he talks about himself he is a bore. He should just keep his mouth shut.

° ° °

He is so stupid that when he was given one of those water-proof, shock-proof, unbreakable and anti-magnetic watches, he lost it.

° ° °

He is an experienced, industrious, ambitious, and often quite picturesque liar.

—Mark Twain

° ° °

Bigot: One who is obstinately and zealously attached to an opinion that you do not entertain.

° ° °

A bore is one who is interesting to a point—the point of departure.

° ° °

He is the kind of highbrow who looks at a sausage and thinks of Picasso.

° ° °

His face looks like a slateful of wrong answers.

—Bugs Baer, *about Firpo*

∘ ∘ ∘

Accept a proverb out of Wisdom's schools:
"Barbers first learn to shave by shaving fools."

—John Wolcot

∘ • ∘

He doesn't know which side of the fence to straddle.

—Bing Crosby

∘ ∘ ∘

He is as fit as a fazzle.

—Ibid

∘ ∘ ∘

He's so creative he doesn't know what he is doing.

∘ ∘ ∘

When arguing with a fool, make sure he isn't doing the same.

∘ ∘ •

He has a heart of gold—like a hard-boiled egg.

∘ ∘ ∘

He is a boneheaded mule who displays characteristic traits.

• ∘ •

Every ass thinks himself worthy to stand with the king's horses.

—John Clarke

• ∘ ∘

What you ass! Must I begin to teach you your letters? For that I shall not need words but a cudgel.

—Cicero

∘ ∘ ∘

He'd be sharper than a serpent's tooth, if he wasn't as dull as ditch water.

—Charles Dickens

• • •

He isn't acting like a fool; he is one.

∘ ∘ ∘

He always puts his foot in his mouth because he neglects the opportunity of keeping his mouth shut.

• ∘ ∘

He always thinks twice before he says nothing.

• ∘ •

He is the kind of a person who belittles everybody to cut them down to his size.

∘ ∘ •

She made a fool out of him, and that was an improvement.

∘ ∘ ∘

Some people think he's a pain in the neck; my opinion of him is even lower.

o o o

He's the kind of a man who pats you on the back to find a soft place to put the knife and then have you arrested for carrying concealed weapons.

o o o

His hat's all right; it's his head that's too small.

o o o

Hotten
Rotten
Forgotten

—Epitaph for John Camden Hotten, G. A. Sala

o o o

He carries such a chip on his shoulders he is always losing his balance.

o o o

To the great he is great; to the fool he's a fool
In the world's dreary desert a crystalline pool,
Where a lion looks in and a lion appears;
But an ass will see only his own ass's ears.

—J. B. Trowbridge

o o o

The ball struck him on the right temple and knocked him cold. He was taken to the Fordham Hospital where X-rays of his head showed nothing.

o o o

He's the kind of guy who will cut your throat behind your back.

o o o

An ass is but an ass though laden with gold.

—Thomas Fuller

o o o

When a jackass brays, no one pays any attention to him, not even other jackasses. But when a lion brays like a jackass, even the lions in the neighborhood may be pardoned for exhibiting a little surprise.

—G.J. Nathan *Testament of a Critic*

o o o

I have been an author for 22 years and an ass for 55.

—Mark Twain

o o o

He is a self-made man and worships his creator.

—John Bright about Disraeli

o o o

He should read the help-wanted ads and he'd be surprised to learn how many positions there are which he is too ignorant, too unattractive and too old to fill.

o o o

He speaks straight from the shoulder. Too bad it doesn't originate a little higher up.

o o o

What besides beef can you expect from an ox?

o o o

He is a philanthropist with other people's money.

o o o

He is so clumsy that if he were to fall on his back he would break his jaw.

o o o

He looks like a giant because he is surrounded by dwarfs.

o o o

If he wants to live a long life, he ought to breathe through his nose and keep his mouth shut.

o o o

His grey hair is a sign of age not wisdom.

o o o

He has a wide mouth and a narrow heart.

o o o

When a bore leaves the room, you feel as if someone came in.

o o o

The community of fools is the biggest community in the world, and the community of crooks is certainly not the smallest.

—*Russian Proverb*

o o o

He has been with dogs so long, he has learned how to bark.

o o o

Of beasts, it is confessed, the ape
Comes nearest us in human shape;
Like man he imitates each fashion.
And malice is his ruling passion.

—Jonathan Swift

o o o

He suffers from headaches because his halo fits so tight.

o o o

He drinks to forget. At the rate he's going he should be suffering from amnesia shortly.

° ° °

He's a man of convictions; and he has served time for every one.

° ° °

His brains are in his feet. He ought to go to a chiropodist for psychoanalysis.

° ° °

He's not only a bachelor, he is the son of a bachelor.

° ° °

She's like a foreign car—she has all her weight in the rear.

° ° °

The best part of his family is underground.

° ° °

She has a figure like an hourglass. It takes that long to figure out what it is.

° ° °

He feels like a cigarette lighter. The spirit is willing but the flash is weak.

° ° °

It seems to me that the Unknown Soldier was my publicity man's last client.

° ° °

She looks like a model for a duffel bag.

° ° °

He is middle-aged; he stopped growing at both ends and has started growing in the middle.

° ° °

His ego keeps on growing without any nourishment.

° ° °

Flattery: Cologne water, to be smelled of but not swallowed.

° ° °

He is a hypocrite who sets good examples when he has an audience.

° ° °

He started singing late in life and didn't stop soon enough.

° ° °

He enjoys a good reputation. He gives publicly and steals privately.

—John Billings

° ° °

He is a hypochondriac and seeks ills for all his pills.

° ° °

He claims to be a self-made man, but he should have called for help.

° ° °

To him life is one round of golf; as soon as he gets out of one hole he gets into another.

° ° °

He is the type of genius who solves a problem you didn't have in a manner you can't understand.

° ° °

He has nothing to hide because he has nothing to show.

° ° °

He may be a good egg but he is slightly cracked.

° ° °

He may have a tiger in the tank but he is a donkey at the wheel.

° ° °

He has such a sharp tongue, he cuts his own throat.

° ° °

Better am I with my cracked foot than you with your crooked mind.

° ° °

A sharp tongue and a dull mind are usually found in the same head.

° ° °

Don't feel sorry for yourself—feel sorry for the folks who have to live with you.

—Elbert Hubbard

° ° °

He thinks he's a wit, but he's only half right.

° ° °

Men are just opposite from guns; the smaller the caliber, the bigger the bore!

° ° °

He claims that what he doesn't know doesn't hurt him, but it sure makes him look stupid.

° ° °

The hotel lobbies may be crowded but there is always room for one bore.

° ° °

He thinks so much of himself he even Xeroxes his paycheck.

° ° °

He looked as if he's stood in line twice when brains were being handed out.

—Christopher Hale, *Exit Screaming*

° ° °

He was more afraid of the world knowing him to be a sinner than God knowing him to be a hypocrite.

° ° °

He belongs to the metallic age—gold in his teeth, silver in his hair and lead in his pants.

° ° °

Gossip can be divided into three categories:
Vest-button type—always popping off.
Vacuum-cleaner type—always picking up dirt.
Liniment type—always rubbing it in.
She's all three rolled into one.

° ° °

If you're ever in California, sir, I do hope you'll come by and use my pool—I'd love to give you some drowning lessons!

—Sammy Davis Jr., to a heckler

° ° °

Fools are ever ready advisers.

° ° °

The Lord made few winged ones but too many that crawl.

° ° °

He is the type of learned person who has read everything, thought of nothing—a walking encyclopedia with no place to go.

° ° °

Most autobiographies are written by corpses.

—S. N. Behrman

° ° °

What was good in aristocracies is long disappeared and what is left is good for nothing.

D. Runes

° ° °

He is a fool who lacks both faith and insight.

° ° °

He is like a blotter—he soaks it all in, but gets it backward.

° ° °

If it be true that one becomes like what he worships, what monsters this world's idol must be!

D. Runes

° ° °

Why don't you write and give me a chance not to reply?

∘ ∘ ∘

You reached me just in time. I was beginning to feel confident again.

∘ ∘ ∘

If things don't improve soon I may have to ask you to stop helping me.

∘ ∘ ∘

He is the biggest spender with his wishes, and the biggest miser with his money.

∘ ∘ ∘

He couldn't sell a glass of water in the Sahara Desert.

—Montagu Glass (1877-1934)

∘ ∘ ∘

He is as smart as a book and just as heartless.

∘ ∘ ∘

His candor is insolence in a full dress suit.

∘ ∘ ∘

A highbrow is a person educated beyond his intelligence.

—B. Matthews

∘ ∘ ∘

They talked together like two egotists,
In conversation made all up of "I's."

—Thomas Hood

∘ ∘ ∘

Dogs and flatterers come in every shape but they all wag one tail.

∘ ∘ ∘

The steps of the dining hall have become considerably worn by the treading of so many heels.

—Professor Bott, Notre Dame

∘ ∘ ∘

He thinks he has an open mind; the truth is that it is only vacant.

∘ ∘ ∘

The question is not where civilization began, but when will it.

∘ ∘ ∘

Whistler, the painter, was at a dinner one night and an awful bore came up to him and said, "Do you know, Mr. Whistler, I passed your house last night."

"Thanks," said Whistler.

∘ ∘ ∘

It usually takes five years for a tree to produce nuts, but this isn't true of a family tree.

∘ ∘ ∘

A million years from now the earth may be filled with creatures who will stoutly deny that they ever descended from man.

° ° °

Quentin Reynolds has a mangy hide which was peeled and nailed to the barn door with the yellow streak glaring for the world to see.

—Westbrook Pegler

° ° °

Reynolds is a celebrity who has fallen in love with himself.

—Westbrook Pegler

° ° °

Reynolds is a fourflusher and a sorry mediocrity.

—Westbrook Pegler

° ° °

This is not the first time someone hearing the name Booth has attacked the President of the United States.

—Quentin Reynolds, about Clare Booth Luce when she attacked the President

° ° °

My God, I hope it's nothing trivial.

—Irwin S. Cobb, when he heard his boss was ill.

° ° °

The world is filled with specialists, if you count those who specialize in fixing the blame.

° ° °

I am an agnostic; I do not pretend to know what many ignorant men are sure of.

—Clarence Darrow

° ° °

A drunkard is like a whiskey bottle, all neck and belly and no head.

° ° °

We load our guns with live ammunition and our minds with blanks.

° ° °

He left home to set the world on fire but returned soon to get some matches.

° ° °

The human race has improved everything except the human race.

—Adlai Stevenson

° ° °

Little monkeys grow up to be big monkeys; little pigs grow

up to be big pigs; but man, wonderful man, can grow up to be either.

—Jim Kelly

o o o

We are moving ahead at twice the speed of sound and half the speed of sense.

o o o

They say kings are made in the image of God. I feel sorry for God if that is what He looks like.

—Frederick the Great

o o o

If man sprang from monkeys he ought to spring once more and make it a safe distance.

o o o

I am a member of the rabble in good standing.

—Westbrook Pegler

o o o

My nobility begins in me, but yours ends in you.

—Iphicrates to Harmodius

o o o

A committee is a body that keeps minutes and wastes hours.

o o o

George M. Cohan wrote to an expensive hotel for reservations. He received an answer which told him they catered to a restricted clientele. They thought he was Jewish. Cohan wired back: "Apparently there has been a mistake on both sides: you thought I was Jewish and I thought you were gentlemen."

o o o

A paper reported that a generous gentleman had donated a new loud-speaker to his church in fond memory of his wife.

o o o

If a man is a small potato, he remains so whether he is boiled, mashed, or French-fried.

—Abba Hillel Silver

o o o

It's not the people in prison who worry me. It's the people who aren't.

—Earl of Arran

o o o

George Bernard Shaw one day received an invitation from a celebrity hunter: "LADY X WILL BE AT HOME THURSDAY BETWEEN 4:00 and 6:00." The author returned the card; underneath he had written: "MR. BERNARD SHAW LIKEWISE."

o o o

The louder he talked of his honor, the faster we counted our spoons.

—Sen. Norris, on Khrushchev's being shocked over the U-2 incident.

o o o

Take the humbug out of the world, and you haven't much left to do business with.

—H. W. Shaw

o o o

I have heard that when Lou Breese went on the radio recently he was responsible for the sale of a quarter-million radios. I sold mine, my brother-in-law sold his . . .

—Joe E. Lewis, about Lou Breese

o o o

No matter how low in value the dollar may fall, it will never fall so low as some people will stoop to get it.

o o o

A cynic is a man who knows the price of everything and the value of nothing.

o o o

He uses statistics as a drunken man uses a lamppost—for support rather than for illumination.

—Andrew Lang

o o o

The cynic is one who never sees a good quality in a man, and never fails to see a bad one. He is the human owl, vigilant in darkness and blind to light, mousing for vermin, but never seeing noble game. The cynic puts all human actions into two bad classes—openly bad and secretly bad.

—Henry Ward Beecher

o o o

Here's to the second nastiest drunk in town.

—Toast made by Rep. Thomas O'Neill to Senator Dodd

o o o

If all the crutches in the world were laid end to end, there still wouldn't be enough for the lame excuses.

—Rep. W. T. Rutherford

o o o

Don't blame it on him. Unfortunately because of the force of gravity, it takes more energy to close the mouth than to open it.

o o o

What used to be TV station breaks are now more like compound fractures.

o o o

I get my exercise by being a pall-bearer to my friends who exercise.

—Chauncey Depew

o o o

The penalty of success is to be bored by people who used to snub you.

—Nancy Lady Astor, First Woman to serve in the House of Commons

o o o

He is a foolish worrier with a circle of inefficient thoughts whirling about a pivot of fears.

o o o

The Supreme Court gave man the right to open his wife's letters but it did not give him the courage.

o o o

Mr. Frick is the only man I know whom Dale Carnegie would have hit in the mouth.

—Bill Veech, about Ford Frick

o o o

Noise proves nothing. Often a hen who has merely laid an egg crackles as if she has laid an asteroid.

—Mark Twain

o o o

This is a dark, dark world, and that is why the Irish are always half-lit.

—Stevenson

o o o

A New England conscience doesn't keep you from doing anything; it just keeps you from enjoying it.

—Mendell

o o o

The more I see of dogs the less I think of men.

—Arsene Houssaye

o o o

The man who has not anything to boast of but his illustrious ancestors is like a potato, the only good belonging to him is underground.

—Sir Thomas Overbury

o o o

Sherry is dull, naturally dull; but it must have taken him a great deal of pain to become what we now see him. Such an excess of stupidity, sir, is not in nature.

—Samuel Johnson, about Sheridan, actor and lecturer

o o o

If man is only a little lower than the angels, the angels should reform.

—M. W. Little

° ° °

He is a man of splendid abilities, but utterly corrupt. He shines and stinks like rotten mackerel by moonlight.

—John Randolph 1773-1833, about Edward Livingston

° ° °

An intellectual is a man who takes more words than necessary to tell more than he knows.

—D. D. Eisenhower, about Stevenson

° ° °

In 1959, when Castro came to power down in Cuba, Ike just sat on his ass, and acted like if he didn't notice what was going on down there, why, maybe Castro would go away or something. Of course what happened, the Russians didn't sit on their asses, and they got him lined up on their side, which is what you have to expect if you've got a goddamn fool in the White House.

—Truman about Ike Eisenhower's Presidency

° ° °

Here lies our sovereign lord the king,
  Whose words no man relies on;
He never says a foolish thing,
  Nor ever does a wise one.

—John Wilmot, Earl of Rochester about Charles II

° ° °

George Bernard Shaw, doing his duty at a benefit affair, asked a dowager to dance. As they waltzed she asked, "Mr. Shaw, whatever made you ask poor little me to dance?" Replied the author, "This is a charity ball, isn't it?"

° ° °

The aristocracy is composed chiefly of asses—asses who talk about horses.

—Heinrich Heine (1797-1856)

° ° °

The right honourable gentleman's smile is like the silver fittings on a coffin.

—Benj. Disraeli, about Sir Robert Peel

° ° °

The public is like a piano. You just have to know what keys to poke.

—Al Capp

° ° °

We cannot put the face on a stamp unless said person is deceased. My suggestion, therefore, is that you drop dead.

—James E. Eay, Postmaster General,
proposed reply to a petitioner who
wanted his picture on a postage stamp.

° ° °

A committee is a group that keeps minutes and loses hours.

—Milton Berle

° ° °

In every generation there has to be some fool who will speak the truth as he sees it.

—Boris Pasternak

° ° °

It will generally be found that those who sneer habitually at human nature, and affect to despise it, are among its worst and least pleasant samples.

—Charles Dickens

° ° °

Money is like manure. If you spread it around, it does a lot of good. But if you pile it up in one place, it stinks like hell.

—Clint Murchinson, Jr., Texas financier

° ° °

The dinosaur's eloquent lesson is that if some bigness is good, an over-abundance of bigness is not necessarily better.

—Eric Johnston, President of U.S. Chamber of Commerce

° ° °

He who will not reason, is a bigot;
He who cannot is a fool;
And he who dares not, is a slave.

—William Drummond

° ° °

This man (Chesterfield) I thought had been a lord among wits; but I find he is only a wit among lords.

—Samuel Johnson

° ° °

My father was a Creole, his father a Negro, and his father a monkey; my family, it seems, begins where yours left off.

—Dumas, on being asked, "Who was your father?"

° ° °

If you haven't got anything good to say about anyone, come and sit by me.

—Alice Roosevelt Longworth

° ° °

An egghead is one who stands firmly on both feet in mid-air

on both sides of an issue.

—Senator Homer Ferguson

o o o

Bernard Shaw hasn't an enemy in the world—and none of his friends like him.

—Oscar Wilde

o o o

A dunghill covered with flowers.

—Henry Watterson, about Henry Ward Beecher

o o o

I rose by sheer military ability to the rank of Corporal.

—Thornton Wilder, Novelist, World War I Army Service

o o o

The place where optimism most flourishes is the lunatic asylum.

—Havelock Ellis (1859-1939)

o o o

Bismarck once remarked to Disraeli, "The Germans have just bought a new country in Africa where Jews and pigs will be tolerated."

Disraeli, without hesitation replied, "Fortunately we are both here."

o o o

"My head today is perfectly barren and you will find me stupid enough, for a friend has been here, and we exchanged ideas."

—Heine

o o o

If a man runs after money, he's money-mad; if he keeps it he's a capitalist; if he spends it, he's a playboy; if he doesn't try to get it, he lacks ambition, if he gets it without working for it, he's a parasite; and if he accumulates it after a life-time of hard work, people call him a fool who never got anything out of life.

—Vic Oliver

o o o

You know what a fan letter is—it's just an inky raspberry.

—Bob Hope

o o o

During a long Texas dry spell an eastern paper stated it was so dry in Texas that the Baptists were sprinkling, the Episcopalians just dusted 'em off and the Presbyterians were taking 'em dirt and all.

o o o

Man was created a little lower than the angels, and has been getting a little lower ever since.

—Josh Billings

o o o

When Albert Schweitzer was asked, "What do you think of civilization?" he answered, "It's a good idea, somebody ought to start it."

o o o

God save me from my friends; I can protect myself from my enemies.

—Marshal De Villars

o o o

In the first place God made idiots; this was practice; then he made school boards.

—Mark Twain

o o o

Reading the epitaphs, our only salvation lies in resurrecting the dead and burying the living.

—Paul Eldridge

o o o

Some folks seem to have descended from the chimpanzee much later than others.

—Kim Hubbard

o o o

Conceit is God's gift to little men.

—Bruce Barton

o o o

Life is an unceasing battle between a man and his enemies, and a woman and her friends.

o o o

Man was made at the end of the week when God was tired.

—Mark Twain

o o o

If you pick up a starving dog and make him prosperous, he will not bite you. This is the principal difference between a dog and a man.

—Ibid

o o o

A government scientist is trying to teach monkeys to smoke cigarettes in a health-research program. The least the animals can do is learn to act like humans. After all, many humans have learned to act like animals.

o o o

If the young man in the back row will remove his hat, I shall continue and point out a concrete example.

—A College Professor

° ° °

Our Heavenly Father invented man because he was disappointed in the monkey.

—Mark Twain

° ° °

I am saddest when I sing. So are those who hear me. They are sadder even than I am.

—Artemus Ward

° ° °

A gossip is a sociologist on a mean and petty scale.

—Woodrow Wilson

° ° °

An athiest cannot find God for the same reason a thief cannot find a policeman.

° ° °

He is just an Empty Mug waiting for the Big Jug to pour wisdom into him.

° ° °

A few more eggheads in the auto industry to supplant the blockheads who designed our recent cars would be in the national interest.

—Bishop G. Gromley Oxnam

° ° °

He who smacks the head of every nail,
Who misses not a trick
Who always hits the bull's eye without fail—
Makes me sick.

—Addison H. Hallock

° ° °

Achilles' mother held him by the heel and dipped him in a stinking river.

° ° °

To most people nothing is more troublesome than the effort of thinking.

—James Bryce (1838-1922)

° ° °

The difference between football and baseball is that in football it's the spectators, not the bases that get loaded.

° ° °

Striking while the iron is hot is all right, but he strikes when the head is hot.

° ° °

He is middle-aged: his narrow waist and broad mind changed places.

° ° °

He can trace his ancestors back to ... to ... well, I don't know exactly who, but he's been descending ever since.

° ° °

If any say that one of thine ears is the ear of an ass, regard it not; if he say so of them both, procure thyself a bridle.

—John Ray

° ° °

Wise men profit more by fools, than fools by wise men; for the wise men avoided the faults of fools, but fools would not imitate the good examples of wise men.

—Plutarch

° ° °

A self-made man is often a big argument against do-it-yourself.

° ° °

Horace Greeley, the great editor, was confronted by a bore, who proclaimed himself to be a self-made man.

"Good," Greeley snapped, "that relieves the Almighty of a terrible responsibility."

° ° °

Hens that make a lot of noise, lay few eggs.

° ° °

Hain't we got all the fools in town on our side? And ain't that a big enough majority in any town?

—Mark Twain

° ° °

Society is now one polished horde,
Formed of two mighty tribes, the
Bores and Bored.

—Lord Byron

° ° °

Mankind fell in Adam, and has been falling ever since, but never touched bottom till it got to Henry Ward Beecher.

—Tom Appleton

° ° °

A communist is like a crocodile. When it opens its mouth you cannot tell whether it is trying to smile or preparing to eat you up.

—Winston Churchill

° ° °

THE FEMALE SPECIES
Introduction

Women! Painters have painted them. Poets have ennobled them. Movies and television have made them glamorous. They are sought, pursued, demanded, and bought. Yet, at the same time, they are the misunderstood sex.

How can men get to understand women? After all, it was God's second thought to create them. Once decided though, He used the best materials in His possession: the white of lilies for cheeks, the red of coral for lips, the blue of heaven for eyes, the black of ravens for hair; and He added the grace of loveliness, kindness and tenderness. Then He mixed all these ingredients together, and out of it came forth woman, beautiful woman.

Yet, with God's all-out effort to produce a masterpiece of creation, He left man with a tremendous problem. Go back in history and you will find that for centuries men have been trying to unravel the mystery of women—with varying degrees of success.

The trouble with men has been that they under-rated women and called them the weaker sex. What a mistake! Listen to Johanan ben Nappaha: "Follow a lion rather than a woman!" Surely, it doesn't sound as though this great sage considered women the weaker sex.

My neighbor claims that women can never be pleased. If they are in business with you and you treat them like men, they get mad. If you treat them like women, your wife gets mad. Either way man loses. Nevertheless, he has decided that he is all for women's Lib. The first thing he wants to do to prove it is to divorce his wife.

My wife is in love with the world. "I love America," she sings. "I love everything American; the people of America, the songs, the literature, and the Bank of America." So, who says women are impractical?

And they can be pretty realistic, believe me. Take this simple dialogue.

"You remind me of the ocean," she said.

"You mean I'm wild, romantic, restless?" he asked.

"Naw, you make me sick."

Along came Martial, the philosopher, evaluator, realist, and penned these lines about women:

A woman is a book, and often found
To prove far better in the SHEETS, than bound;
No wonder, then, some students take delight,
Above all things, to STUDY IN THE NIGHT.

When all is said and done, men have found pros and cons with regard to women—sometimes the same man finds both. Dumas wrote: "It is often woman who inspires us with the great things that she will prevent us from accomplishing." And George Eliot, with tongue in cheek, counseled: "I'm not denying that women are foolish. God Almighty made 'em to match the men."

As for me, I'm all for women. After all, some of my best friends are women. I go along with Lincoln who penned these lines:

Whatever spiteful fools may say,
Each jealous ranting yelper,
No woman ever went astray,
Without a man to help her.

And so what do you think about women? Do you agree with Pigault-Lebrum who wrote: "Those who always speak *well* of women do not know them enough; and those who always speak *ill* of them do not know them at all."

Come on, men, own up! Without woman the two extremes of life would be without succor, and the middle without pleasure. Three cheers for George Bernard Shaw who wisely wrote: "Woman reduces us all to a common denominator."

Read on!

THE FEMALE SPECIES

That woman is a regular clothes horse. When she puts on her clothes she looks like a horse.

o o o

It is amazing what she can get away with and still keep her amateur standing.

o o o

In lying, men are commoners, women are aristocrats.

—Abel Hermant

o o o

A man of straw is worth more than a woman of gold.

—John Florie

o o o

A thing that is better lost than found—a woman.
—Richard Brome

° ° °

The more women the more witchcraft.
—Rabbi Hillel (Pirke Aboth)

° ° °

Men have many faults, poor women have but two,
There's nothing right they say, and nothing right they do.
—Cheales, Proverbial Folk-Lore

° ° °

There is no sea-wave without salt;
There is no woman without fault.
—John Hay

° ° °

There is no such thing as picking out the best woman; one is worse than another.
—Plautus

° ° °

A woman's tongue, three inches long, can kill a man six feet high.
—Champion

° ° °

A woman's sword is her tongue, and she does not let it rust.
—Champion

° ° °

She is the kind of a woman who always enters a room voice first.

° ° °

If all the cars in America were placed end to end, some woman would pull over and try to pass them.

° ° °

The only time one woman stops talking is when her mother starts.

° ° °

Man was created first so that he would have a chance to say something.

° ° °

She has a pretty little head. For a head, it's pretty little.

° ° °

The only thing holding up her dress is a city ordinance.

° ° °

Women get along fine; they live off the fatheads of the land.

° ° °

Her flattery makes you feel like a pancake that's just had the syrup poured on it.

o o o

Women can convince you that they're going places when they're really taking you.

o o o

A woman recently advertised: "Woman with income tax blank would like to meet man with income."

o o o

I know a woman who has more crust than a pie factory.

o o o

She claims she's just turned thirty—it must have been a "U" turn.

o o o

The woman who claims to be around 30 is right; it's nearly the second time around.

o o o

She talks 50% faster than anyone can listen.

o o o

I find more bitter than death the woman, whose heart is snares and nets, and her hands are as bands.

Eccles. 7:26

o o o

A wise man saw a hunter conversing with a woman, and he remarked: Take care that you don't become the game.

—Hasdai, Ben HaMelek VeHaNazir

o o o

When you find an all-white raven, you'll find also a virtuous woman.

o o o

Women lie even when they are silent.

—Lipperheide

o o o

A woman's wisdom is only at her spindle.

—Eliezer ben Hyrcanus

o o o

O woman! woman! What a benefactor to his race is that man who frees us from your chains!

—Heine, *Baths of Lucca*, 1828

o o o

Every woman has her weapons on her.

The Talmud

o o o

From a woman did sin originate, and because of her we all must die.

—*Apocrypha: Ben Sira, 25, 24*

Let the Law be burned rather than entrusted to a woman.

—Eliezer ben Hyrcanus

° ° °

Women: The ones you want are always the wrong age or the wrong height or something, and the ones who are after you are always the ones you don't want.

° ° °

My wife and I have two closets
 We share to the best of our powers.
One closet is strictly for HER clothes,
 The other is strictly for OURS.

—Leo Hershfeld

° ° °

Women are more generous than men especially when what they are giving away isn't money.

° ° °

Some women make a beeline
For every scrawny, mangy feline.
Love to keep and feed and carry one.
I'm lucky I didn't marry one.

° ° °

Women feed their hair. They use milk for setting hair, club soda for tinting, salt in the shampoo for oil hair, and salad dressing for a conditioner. Is it any wonder that an inspired poet wrote (Leo Hershfeld):

It's not the beauty parlor where
You ladies need to take your hair.
No, it's the kitchen, nothing greater,
With head inside refrigerator.

° ° °

Love-making hasn't changed in a thousand years. They tell us that Greek maidens used to sit and listen to a lyre all evening, too.

° ° °

When the Creator gave out brains, she thought He said trains —and she missed her's!

° ° °

When he gave out good looks, she thought He said books—and she didn't want any.

° ° °

When He said noses, she thought He said roses—and she ordered a big red one.

o o o

Boy! Is my wife a mess!

o o o

According to evolutionists, it took nature millions of years to make a man out of a monkey. A woman can reverse the process in a jiffy.

o o o

When a woman dies, people find out how many children she had.

o o o

Long hair and short senses are characteristics of a woman.

o o o

Hell can lie between the lashes of a beautiful woman's eyes.

—*Sefer ha-Hinukh*

o o o

Women are ready to trust men—if they'll put their money in trust for them.

o o o

She claims she's the boss in the house and that he's a nothing. This makes her a boss over nothing.

o o o

Fabia Dollabella, saying she was 30 years old, received this reply from Cicero, "It must be true, for I have heard it these twenty years."

o o o

Some girls fall head over heels in love with a fellow, while others go ahead and fall in love with heels.

o o o

Standing near her makes you realize what a source of earitation she is.

o o o

Behind every successful man is a good woman—and the chances are she'll catch him.

o o o

What women hear is never as exciting as what they overhear.

o o o

A woman's heart and her tongue are not relatives.

—Robert Greene

o o o

Women strive for the last word.

—Thomas Fuller

° ° °

Her tongue was perfect and never halted at a word.

° ° °

Vitality in a woman is a blind fury of creation.

—George Bernard Shaw

° ° °

Let men say whate'er they will,
Woman, woman rules them still.

—Isaac Bickerstaff

° ° °

A nut tree, an ass, and a woman are bound together by the same law: None of the three will do well if the beatings cease.

—Cognatus, Adagia, 1560

° ° °

Women are liars since the world began.

—John Masefield, *The Widow in the Bye Street*

° ° °

Dames lie about anything—just for practice.

° ° °

Women make lies out of truth
And out of a molehill their mountains.

—Phyllis McGinley

° ° °

Women's light thoughts make their husbands' heavy heads.

—Robert Greene

° ° °

I expect that woman will be the last thing civilized by man.

—George Meredith

° ° °

In point of morals the average woman is, even for business, too crooked.

—Stephen Leacock, *The Woman Question*

° ° °

One man among a thousand have I found; but a woman among all those have I not found.

—*Proverbs*

° ° °

A silent woman is a gift from the lord.

—*Apocrypha: Ben Sira 25:15*

° ° °

A storm, however sudden, is yet preceded by a warning breeze; but how can one guard against a woman's temper?

—Boerne, *Der Narr*

° ° °

A woman will uncover a pot to see what her neighbor's cooking.

—*The Mishna*

° ° °

When God was about to create Eve, He considered well from what part of Adam to create her. Said He: "I will not use the head, lest she be swell-headed; not the eye, lest she be a coquette, not the ear, lest she be an eavesdropper; not the mouth, lest she be a gossip; not the heart, lest she be prone to jealousy; not the hand, lest she be light-fingered; not the foot, lest she be a gadabout; I shall make her from a hidden part of man, that she be modest." Yet in spite of all the precautions, she is subject to all these faults.

° ° °

Women's styles may change, but their designs remain the same.

—*Look Magazine*

° • °

Women are fickle.

—Simeon ben Yohai

° ° °

Women are fond of talking.

—Nathan. *T:Berakot, 48b*

° ° °

Woman's love is writ in water,
Woman's faith is traced in sand.

—William Edmonstoune Aytoun

° ° °

You see, dear, it is not true that woman was made from man's rib; she was really made from his funny bone.

—Sir James Matthew Barrie

° ° °

I wish Adam had died with all his ribs in his body.

—Dion Boucicault

° ° °

Lost is our freedom,
When we submit to women so:
Why do we need them,
When in their best they work our woe?

—Thomas Campion

° ° °

Woman is often fickle; very foolish is he who trusts them.

—Francis I

° ° °

A beautiful and chaste woman is the perfect workmanship of God, the true glory of angels, the rare miracle of earth, and the sole wonder of the world.

—George Hermes

° ° °

Women have tongues of craft, and hearts of guile,
They will, they will not; fools that on them trust;
For in their speech is death, hell in their smile.

—Torquato Tasso

° ° °

Frailty, thy name is Woman!

—*Hamlet*, Act I, Scene 2, Shakespeare

° ° °

A woman may wear pearls around her neck, though she have stones on her heart.

° ° °

Women are nine times more talkative than men.

° ° °

May God protect you from bad women: protect yourself against good ones.

° ° °

Women? You suffer before you get them, while you have them, and after you lose them.

—Sholom Aleichem

° ° °

The Kinsey report proved just one thing: Women like to talk.

° ° °

Three women can keep a secret if two are dead.

° ° °

A horse is usually a horse; but a woman can also be a nag.

° ° °

Arguing with a woman is like trying to read a newspaper in a high wind.

° ° °

When a man has a birthday, sometimes he takes a day off; when a woman has one, she takes at least a year off.

° ° °

The only way to have the last word with a woman is to apologize.

° ° °

Hurricanes cause a lot of trouble. They make a lot of noise, do a lot of damage, and nobody can control them—no wonder they named them after women.

° ° °

Never any good came out of female domination.

—Martin Luther, *Table Talk*

° ° °

Women, you know, do seldom fail
To make the stoutest men turn tail.

—Samuel Butler

° ° °

"Why did God make you women so beautiful and so dumb?" asked an irate husband of his wife.

Sweetly she replied, "God made women beautiful so you men would love us, and He made us dumb so we could love you men."

° ° °

Women's styles may change but their designs remain the same.

° ° °

If she could only make her hands move as quickly as her tongue, what wonders she could perform.

° ° °

If she has horse sense, she will probably turn into a nag.

° ° °

Women who carry tales make monkeys of themselves.

° ° °

She's a person who goes places and the sooner the better.

° ° °

A man knocks before he enters, a woman after she leaves.

° ° °

A woman stands a better chance of catching a man if she keeps her trap closed.

° ° °

I am glad that I am not a man, for then I should have to marry a woman.

—Mme. De Stael

° ° °

When men and women die, as poets sung
His heart's the last part moves,—her last, the tongue.

—Benjamin Franklin, *Poor Richard's Almanac*

° ° °

Women are getting dumber as they grow smarter.

—Mary Garden

° ° °

Men, some to business, some to pleasure take;
But every woman is at heart a rake.

° ° °

Women, like men, will fade away,
Their eyes grow dim, their teeth decay,
But while they breathe the vital gale,
'Tis strange their tongues should never fail.

—Henry Tufts

° ° °

In preferring the company of ladies to that of the bottle, I only exchange a headache for a heartache.

—James Kirke Paulding

° ° °

Women, who are, beyond all doubt, the mothers of all mischief, also nurse that babe to sleep when he is too noisy.

—Richard Doddridge Blackmore (1825-1900)

° ° °

Not all women are guilty of repeating gossip. There must be a few who start it.

° ° °

God made women without a sense of humor so they could love men instead of laughing at them.

° ° °

Beneath this stone a lump of clay
    Lies Arabella Young
Who on the 21st of May
    Began to hold her tongue.

—On a tombstone, 1771

° ° °

She is such a gossip that when you wind her up, she runs someone down.

° ° °

Some little girls grow up to be kittenish, she grew up to be a cat.

° ° °

She has a voice like the throttling of cats . . . one verse from her would clear a parish.

—Brendan Behan

° ° °

Women are pictures; men are problems. If you want to know what a woman really means, look at her, don't listen to her.

—Oscar Wilde

° ° °

When women kiss, it always reminds me of prize-fighters shaking hands.

—H.L. Mencker

° ° °

Women have no minor voices.

° ° °

Women wreck the matrimonial bark with their matrimonial barking.

° ° °

Women believe in free speech and certainly are free enough with their own.

° ° °

There are three quick ways of spreading news: telephone, telegraph, and women.

° ° °

Women can sling dirt faster than gravediggers.

° ° °

Blonde or brunette, this rhyme applies,
Happy is he who knows them not.

° ° °

Whilst Adam slept, Eve from his side arose:
Strange his first sleep should be his last repose.

° ° °

A man never knows how to say good-bye; a woman never knows when to say it.

—Helen Rowland

° ° °

Show me a genuine case of platonic friendship, and I will show you two old or homely faces.

—Austin O'Malley

° ° °

It takes one woman twenty years to make a man of her son, and another woman twenty minutes to make a fool of him.

—Helen Rowland

° ° °

We have medicines to make women speak; we have none to make them keep silence.

—Anatole France, *The Man Who Married A Dumb Wife*

° ° °

A public speaking lady is like a dog standing on its hind legs. It never is well done; in fact, one is surprised that it is done at all.

—Dr. Samuel Johnson

° ° °

The whole world is strewn with snares, traps, gins, and pitfalls for the capture of men by women.

—George Bernard Shaw

° ° °

Nature abhors a virgin—a frozen asset.

—Clare Boothe Luce

° ° °

All women's dresses are merely variations between the eternal struggle between the admitted desire to dress and the unadmitted desire to undress.

—Lin Yutang

° ° °

Some women get pearls from oysters, but she gets diamonds from shrimps.

° ° °

She is a well-reared girl and cannot afford to wear slacks.

° ° °

But what is woman? Only one of nature's agreeable blunders.

—Cowley

° ° °

A rag and a bone and a hank of hair.

—Kipling, *The Vampire*

° ° °

Regard the society of women as a necessary unpleasantness of social life, and avoid it as much as possible.

—Tolstoy *Diary*

° ° °

The only silent women are those who have no tongues.

° ° °

She picks up more dirt with the telephone than anyone else does with a vacuum cleaner.

° ° °

The way to fight a woman is with your hat. Grab it and run.

—John Barrymore

° ° °

A woman is only a woman, but a cigar is a smoke.

—Rudyard Kipling

° ° °

Ask a woman's advice, and whate'er she advise,
Do the very reverse, and you're sure to be wise.

—Thomas Moore

° ° °

Men seldom make passes
At girls who wear glasses.

—Dorothy Parker

° ° °

Here's to women: So much like a clock—pretty hands, pretty

face, pretty movement, and hard to regulate when they get out of order.

—Arthur L. Kaser

o o o

There are three classes into which all elderly women that I ever knew were to be divided: first, the dear old soul; second, that old woman; third, that old witch.

—Samuel T. Coleridge

o o o

Madam, before you flatter a man so grossly to his face, you should consider whether your flattery is worth his having.

—Ben Johnson

o o o

The surest way to hit a woman's heart is to take aim kneeling.

—Douglas Jerrold

o o o

One wife is necessary, a second is a luxury, a third wife is a waste, and a fourth is punishment.

—Ahmand Irshad

o o o

Many a man has fallen in love with a girl in a light so dim, he would not have chosen a suit by it.

—Maurice Chevalier

o o o

To enjoy women at all one must manufacture an illusion and envelop them with it; otherwise, they would not be endurable.

—George Jean Nathan

o o o

A ship is always referred to as a "she" because it cost so much to keep her in paint.

—Admiral Chester Nimitz
N.Y. Times, May 24, 1959

o o o

She is the only woman I know who drinks pot.

—Bob Hope, after drinking
strong tea with Alice Roosevelt
Longworth

o o o

Woman would be more charming if you could fall into her arms without falling into her hands.

—Amerose Bierce

o o o

When she's with me, I feel alone.

o o o

FAMILY LIFE
Introduction

Someone once remarked that marriage is for nuts and bolts. There seems to be some confusion. It was Oscar Wilde who pointed out that "Nowadays all the married men live like bachelors, and all the bachelors like married men."

The trouble is that fun has been taken out of marriage. For a buck twenty-five any married couple can purchase a fourteen-page, large-sized, single-spaced pamphlet telling you how to evaluate your own marriage. "Discover your real problems," it states in bold type on the cover. On the inside pages some 1,000 diagnostic questions are asked, guaranteed to *give* you marital difficulties if you don't have them already.

And then take a look at some of the book titles: *How to Be Happy And Married*, as though it was a tremendous difficulty. *Getting Mileage Out of Your Mate*, as though you were purchasing a car. *Marriage Is a Scavenger Hunt* is the title of another book. A friend of mine quietly stated that for him marriage was a state of hate.

To marry or not to marry, that is the question. And Thomas Bailey Aldrich supplies part of the answer when he writes:

> Some weep because they part,
> And languish broken-hearted,
> And others-O my heart!—
> Because they never parted.

Did you know that there are now courses in marriage? I wonder how they rate the students? And who is the teacher? And what is the syllabus? And who gives the tests? My idea is to call in a student and tell him outright: Marriage has many thorns, but the roses are beautiful and sweet. Now go out and pick the roses, not the thorns.

What married people need is a sense of humor. Laugh at yourself and with one another. If you can do this, your marriage will last much longer. Take Smith and Jones. They met on the way to work. Said Smith: "What do you say, we get our wives together tonight and have a swell evening?"

"Swell idea," Jones replied. "Where'll we leave them?"

Of course, it's meant in fun.

Marriage is a wonderful institution. I recall a clergyman, while engaged in sermonizing before a group of students, asked one boy for his definition of matrimony. The reply was quite startling: "A place of punishment where some souls suffer for a time before they can go to heaven." So, who says children are not bright?

God help the man who won't marry until he finds a perfect woman, and God help him still more if he finds her.

Seriously, for one moment anyhow, I might say that two people who have selected each other out from all the available partners in the human species, expecting to be each other's mutual comfort and entertainment have, in that action, bound themselves to be good humored, affable, discreet, forgiving, patient, and joyful, with respect to each other's frailties and perfections, to the end of their lives.

"Marriage!" said Ibsen. "Nothing else demands so much from a man." To counter this bit of wisdom, Mary Buckley says, "Husbands are awkward things to deal with. Even keeping them in hot water will not make them tender."

Throw away the Marital IQ. Get rid of all the DO IT YOURSELF books. Put romance back in your life and learn to laugh.

So, let's get together and poke a bit of fun at marriage. Let's have a few laughs. After all, before you married you kept both eyes wide open. Now that you are married, keep at least one of them shut—and laugh along with me.

FAMILY LIFE

My wife is like an angel, always harping on something.

o o o

A husband who says his wife can't take a joke forgets himself.

o o o

My wife opens nothing more by mistake than her mouth.

o o o

"How come," asked the wife of her husband, "that you know so much about banking, economics and money, and have so little of it?"

o o o

My husband is not entirely useless; he can serve as a horrible example.

o o o

Wife: "I was given a sense of humor to console me for what you are."

o o o

Husband: "It was love at first sight, but I should have taken a second look."

o o o

My husband growls all day! No wonder he's dog-tired all night.

o o o

Wife: "What is the difference between direct and indirect taxes?"

Husband: "The same as the difference between your asking me for money and going through my pockets when I'm asleep."

o o o

When my husband works, he doesn't think, and when he thinks he doesn't work.

o o o

My husband tried his hand at everything and failed; now he ought to try his head.

o o o

"Those cynics among you," intoned the voice from the pulpit, "who are worried over where the younger generation is headed, might well consider very seriously where it came from."

o o o

Fathers are what give daughters away to other men who aren't good enough for them—so they can have grandchildren who are smarter than anybody's.

o o o

"Always tell your wife the truth," advised the marriage counselor who sells dog houses as a sideline.

o o o

The little girl ended her evening prayers with: "And please watch over daddy, and while You're watching, You'd better keep an eye on Mama, too."

o o o

A genius: a stupid kid with very happy grandparents.

o o o

"Do you believe in the devil?" asked one girl of another.

"Of course not!" came back the immediate reply. "It's just like Santa Claus—he's your father."

o o o

My grandmother reads the Bible so much because she is preparing for her finals.

o o o

Psychiatrists say that girls tend to marry men like their fathers. That's the reason why mothers cry so much at weddings.

o o o

I don't care that my husband gets so angry, but for some reason anger makes his mouth work faster than his mind.

o o o

My wife is like a river. Whatever is in her comes out at the mouth.

o o o

The height of something or other is a dumb girl turning a deaf ear to a blind date.

o o o

The father who does not go to church because there are so many hypocrites there, can be found Sunday morning on a golf course full of them.

o o o

A woman never really makes a fool of a man—she merely directs the performance.

o o o

Every busy man should have a wife, so he won't waste so much time making up his mind about things.

o o o

Alimony is the take from a mistake.

o o o

No domestic science course is necessary to enable my wife to make a traffic jam.

o o o

An ambitious wife is the power behind the drone.

o o o

My wife goes to pieces at the slightest provocation because probably she was never assembled properly in the first place.

o o o

My wife is so quick to draw that she shoots my bank balance all to pieces.

o o o

All tiny babies are angels. But their wings grow shorter as their legs grow longer.

o o o

Behind every man there's a woman—and she usually catches him, too.

o o o

One way to put your boss in good humor is—do the dishes for her!

o o o

The last word in an argument is what a wife has. Anything a husband says after that is the beginning of another argument.

∘ ∘ ∘

There is one advantage in being married: you can't make a fool of yourself without knowing it.

∘ ∘ ∘

Most men are like worms in the grass; they wriggle around awhile—then some chicken grabs them.

∘ ∘ ∘

A bachelor is a man whose mind is filled with obstinacy and whose soul is filled with suspicion.

∘ ∘ ∘

Husbands are of three varieties: prizes, surprises, and consolation prizes.

∘ ∘ ∘

Making a husband out of a man is one of the highest arts known to civilization. It requires science, patience, persistence, faith, hope, and charity.

∘ ∘ ∘

"When my husband speaks in public," said the woman proudly, "I tremble."

The husband, sitting nearby, commented, "And when my wife speaks in private, I tremble."

∘ ∘ ∘

A teacher was once asked, "Why didn't God create Eve before Adam?"

"That's very simple to understand," replied the teacher. "Because it's dangerous to start with a woman."

∘ ∘ ∘

A coat of paint sometimes makes an old house look new, but not an old woman.

∘ ∘ ∘

The millionaire's wife hovered at her husband's sickbed as the doctor conducted his examination. Afterward, in the hall, she asked, "Is there any hope, doctor?"

"That depends," said the physician. "Just what are you hoping for?"

∘ ∘ ∘

The days just prior to marriage are like a snappy introduction to a tedious book.

—Wilson Mizner

∘ ∘ ∘

Marriage is neither heaven nor hell; it is simply purgatory.

—Abraham Lincoln

∘ ∘ ∘

When billing and cooing results in matrimony, the billing

always comes after the cooing.

—Tom Masson

° ° °

One good husband is worth two good wives; for the scarcer things are, the more they're valued.

—Benjamin Franklin

° ° °

My wife tells me that a successful marriage involves give and take. Ours is successful. I give in and she takes over.

° ° °

She had this placed on the tombstone at her husband's grave:

"Without you I cannot bear to live."

She remarried within the year and then added one additional word:

"Alone."

° ° °

Alimony is like buying oats for a dead horse.

—Arthur (Bugs) Baer

° ° °

Alimony is a system by which one pays for the mistake of two.

—John Garland Pollard

° ° °

The Don Juans among men and the light-o-loves among women are afraid of marriage.

—Alfred Adler

° ° °

Men marry because they are tired—women because they are curious—both are disappointed.

—Oscar Wilde

° ° °

The luckiest man was Adam—he had no mother-in-law.

—Shalom Aleichem

° ° °

Parents wonder why the streams are bitter when they themselves have poisoned the fountain.

—John Locke

° ° °

A lot of homes are ruined by inferior desecrators.

—Frank Lloyd Wright

° ° °

It's a pity to waste a college education on high school graduates who already know everything.

° ° °

When adults act like children they are silly. When children act like adults they are delinquents.

° ° °

A ten-year-old, riding along the highway with his parents, remarked, "Look at the bull-boards."

° ° °

The first half of our lives is ruined by our parents and the second half by our children.

—Clarence Darrow

° ° °

It has been said that paternity is a career imposed on you one fine morning without any inquiry as to your fitness for it. That is why there are so many fathers who have children but so few children who have fathers.

—Adlai Stevenson

° ° °

The thing that impresses me most about America is the way parents obey their children.

—Duke of Windsor

° ° °

There are no illegitimate children—only illegitimate parents.

—Judge Leon R. Yankeich

° ° °

The trouble with your children is that when they're not being a lump in the throat, they're being a pain in the neck.

—Cy N. Peace

° ° °

Public schools are the nurseries of vice and immorality.

—Henry Fielding

° ° °

Abraham Lincoln,
his hand and pen;
he will be good, but
God knows when.

—Lincoln, in a childhood copy book

° ° °

Out of the mouths of babes come words we shouldn't have said in the first place.

° ° °

Simply having children doesn't make mothers.

—John A. Shedd

° ° °

My mother is a person who is never outspoken.

° ° °

You never hear of anyone giving the groom a shower. They figure he is all washed up anyway.

o o o

He worships the ground she walks on, and why not? A farm that size is not to be sneezed at.

o o o

To damage some men's brains you would have to hit their wives on the head.

o o o

As far as housework is concerned, my wife likes to do nothing better.

o o o

The one trouble with my wife who does nothing is that she complains that because of it she can't stop and rest.

o o o

Judge: "Why did you desert your wife?"
Husband: "I'm not a deserter; I'm a refugee."

o o o

They've been married twenty years, and he loves her still.

o o o

She claims they are compatible; they both love to fight.

o o o

Before they were married, he was well-off, but he didn't know it then.

o o o

An optimist is a single person contemplating marriage; a pessimist is a married man contemplating it.

o o o

When a divorced man marries a divorced woman, there are four minds in the bed.

—The Talmud

o o o

My wife has a narrow mind and a big mouth to match.

o o o

My wife thinks she is a big wheel; take the air out of her and all that's left is a flat tire.

o o o

If ignorance is bliss, why doesn't she jump with joy.

o o o

Any wickedness, only not the wickedness of a woman!

—Ben Sira

o o o

No woman ever faithful hold
Unless she ugly be and old.

—Immanuel, *Mahberot*

° ° °

My wife is doing fine with her driving lessons; the road is beginning to turn when she does.

° ° °

Many an old hen makes a goose of herself trying to look like a chicken.

° ° °

Everybody makes mistakes but my wife lends assistance.

° ° °

My wife's mouth is like a good hotel—open all year 'round.

° ° °

Looking at her husband, she exclaimed, "I wish I had loved and lost!"

° ° °

My wife is over-dressed; she is wrapped up in herself.

° ° °

My wife thinks she is a big shot because she is always exploding.

° ° °

Isadora Duncan, the great dancer, once wrote to George Bernard Shaw and suggested, or so it is rumored, "We two ought to have a child, so it could inherit my beauty and your brains."

Shaw wrote back. "Madam, I am flattered—but suppose it turned out to have my beauty and your brains?"

° ° °

Two teardrops were floating down the river of time, and one said to the other. "Why were you shed?" And the little teardrop said, "I am the tear of a young girl who loved a young man and lost him. Whose tear are you?"

And the other teardrop replied, "I am the tear of the girl who got him."

—Ilka Chase

° ° °

A bachelor never quite gets over the idea that he is a thing of beauty and a boy forever.

—Helen Rowland

° ° °

A bachelor is a souvenir of some woman who found a better one at the last minute.

° ° °

When Monsieur Dubois was advised that all he had to do was to look his misfortunes right in the face and laugh at them, he replied, "I wouldn't dare. Neither my wife nor my mother-in-law has a sense of humor."

° ° °

Distrust all mothers-in-law. They are completely unscrupulous in what they say in court. The wife's mother is always more prejudiced against the husband than even the most ill-treated wife. If I had my way, I am afraid I would abolish mothers-in-law entirely.

—Sir Geoffrey Wrangham

° ° °

A woman will almost never tell you the truth, while most men defendants will. Women have a furtive, concealing nature, and to some extent they're pathological liars who can conceive of situations that never existed.

—James D.C. Murray

° ° °

First, there is the rocket-boosted mother-in-law . . . She is queen of the melodrama when the acts of self-sacrifice and martyrdom go unnoticed and unrewarded. Her banner is the tear-stained hanky. She is as phony as a colic cure, transparent as a soap bubble. And as harmless as a barracuda. But she is really more wretched than wicked and needs more help than she can give.

—Abigail Van Buren, *McCalls,* 1962

° ° °

The graveyards are full of women whose houses were so spotless you could eat off the floor. Remember the second wife always has a maid.

—Helloise Cruse

° ° °

She was a free-lance castrater.

—Jules Feiffer, Humorist

° ° °

There are only about twenty murders a year in London and not all are serious—some are just husbands killing their wives.

—Commander G.H. Hatherill, *Scotland Yard News*

° ° °

Women do not talk all day:
It only seems to sound that way.

° ° °

Don't marry for money; you can borrow it cheaper.

° ° °

Isn't it amazing how many things there are that wives would rather have than money.

—Husband, upon observing a wife on a shopping tour

° ° °

She is making her own marital grave with all those digs she gives him.

° ° °

A hotel manager received this letter: "Have you suitable accommodations where I can put up with my wife?"

° ° °

News item: They could find no reason for the suicide. He was unmarried.

° ° °

When I put the ring on my finger, I didn't realize that it was the smallest handcuff in the world.

° ° °

I've sometimes thought of marrying—and then I've thought again.

—Noel Coward

° ° °

They stood before the altar and supplied
The fire themselves in which their fat was fried.

—Ambrose Bierce

° ° °

You may write it on his tombstone
You may cut it on his card,
That a young man married
Is a young man marred.

—Kipling

° ° °

A coquette is a woman without a heart, who makes a fool of a man that hasn't got any head.

—Mme. Deluzy

° ° °

Hollywood is a place where movie stars are marrying more and enjoying it less.

° ° °

Telling lies is a fault in a boy, an art in a lover, an accomplishment in a bachelor, and second nature in a married woman.

—Helen Rowland

° ° °

"By whom?" asked the man in surprise, when told that his wife was outspoken.

° ° °

Arguing with my wife is like this. "I came! I saw! I concurred!"

o o o

The man who gives in when he is right is spineless, weak, and probably married.

o o o

Marriage they tell us, is made of three rings—engagement ring, wedding ring, and suffering.

o o o

You might just as well let your wife know who is the boss right from the start. Why kid yourself?

o o o

"My husband is a bookworm."
"You're lucky; mine is just the ordinary kind."

o o o

It's a funny thing, when he didn't have anything to worry about, he went off and got married.

o o o

Love is like an onion, you taste with delight, and when it's gone you wonder whatever made you bite!

o o o

A yawn is nature's way of letting men open their mouths.

o o o

The marriage rate is still going up, which seems to indicate that this country is still the home of the brave.

o o o

Leisure time is when your wife can't find you.

o o o

My wife not only kept her girlish figure; she doubled it.

o o o

Colonel Washington Cloud, a famous Southern lawyer, was fond as the next man of a drop of bourbon. As he tottered home one night, a neighbor woman stopped him in the street and said, "If I were your wife, I'd poison you!"
Looking straight at her, he answered, "Madam, if you were my wife, I'd take it."

o o o

Women have recently been placed at a disadvantage: Man can now travel faster than sound.

o o o

She is the kind of a gossip who will never tell a lie if the truth will do as much damage.

o o o

Grandpa says every married man should try to forget his mistakes. There's no use in two people remembering the same thing.

o o o

My wife thinks by the inch, talks by the yard; I'd like to move her by the foot.

o o o

Most women know how to say nothing; few know when.

o o o

Husband: I saw Jason Briggs downtown today and he didn't even speak to me. I guess he thinks I'm not his equal."

Wife: "Why, that stupid, brainless, conceited, good-for-nothing moron! You certainly are his equal."

o o o

Marriage is a tyranny, a mortification of man's natural instincts. Man needs a multiplicity of relationships.

—Frederico Fellini

o o o

My wife is the kind of a person who not only keeps you from being lonely, but makes you wish you were.

o o o

Marriage begins with a prince kissing an angel. It ends with a bald-headed man looking across the table at a fat woman.

o o o

After all is said and done, it's usually the wife who has said it, and the husband who has done it.

—Sammy Kaye

o o o

A married man is a man with a past, while a bachelor is a man with a future.

—George Bernard Shaw

o o o

Sometimes a man pulls the wool over the wife's eyes with the wrong yarn.

o o o

One should always be in love. That is the reason one should never marry.

—Oscar Wilde

o o o

My wife loves to make a career out of her misfortunes.

o o o

Bigamy is having one wife too many—monogamy is identical.

o o o

Masochism has an intimate relationship with femininity.

—Sigmund Freud

° ° °

The first half of our lives is ruined by our parents and the second half by our children.

—Clarence Darrow

° ° °

Romantic love is a form of temporary insanity.

—Naromji

° ° °

Without marriage there would be no illegitimate children.

—Naromji

° ° °

Matrimony: I hate it because it is the grave of love.

—Casanova

° ° °

Love is the child of illusion and the parent of disillusion.

—Miguel DeUnamuno

° ° °

Love is the most radical way of turning a man into an idiot.

—Salvatore Dali

° ° °

On the publication of Lord Chesterfield's letters to his natural son: "They teach the morals of a whore, and the manners of a dancing master."

° ° °

A woman will buy anything she thinks a store is losing money on.

—Kin Hubbard

° ° °

My wife is the kind of a girl that makes men jump into rivers and climb mountains—she's a woman driver!

° ° °

An optimist is a husband who goes down to the marriage bureau to see if his license has expired.

° ° °

"Dear Alice," wrote the young man. "I'm getting so forgetful, that while I remember proposing to you last night, I forget whether you said 'Yes' or 'No'."

"Dear Bob," Alice answered. "So glad to hear from you. I know I said 'No' to someone last night, but I had forgotten just who it was."

° ° °

My wife reads just enough to keep herself misinformed.

° ° °

"Does m-i-r-a-g-e spell marriage?" a child asked of her father.

"Yes, my child," was the terse reply.

° ° °

A woman free with her charms once asked Robert Benchley to help her write her epitaph. He offered to help and wrote these words: "AT LAST SHE SLEEPS ALONE."

° ° °

When Milton was blind, he married a shrew. One of his friends called her a rose. "I am no judge of colors," replied Milton, "and it may be so, for I feel the thorns daily."

° ° °

In breaking his engagement, a young man wrote. "I could not love thee, dear, so much."

° ° °

Whether you wind up with a nest egg or a goose egg, depends a lot on the kind of chick you married.

° ° °

Never get married while you're going to college; it's hard to get a start if a prospective employer finds you've already made one mistake.

—K. Hubbard

° ° °

The difference between a wife and a mistress is the difference between night and day.

—Harry Hershfield

° ° °

The ability to make love frivolously is the chief characteristic which distinguishes human beings from the beasts.

—Heywood Broun

° ° °

My father never raised a hand to any of his children, except in self-defense.

—Fred Allen

° ° °

Monogamy is for the birds, and there are only six of the eight thousand six hundred and fourteen species of birds on earth who follow it.

° ° °

My wife can dye her hair but she cannot change her character.

° ° °

Advocates and practitioners of the unnatural and inhuman crime of monogamy are selfish, cruel, jealous, joyless, hypocritical, and stupid.

—Jim Moran

o o o

"I chase girls," confided the old man, "but I can't remember why when I catch up with them."

o o o

For twenty years my wife and I were ecstatically happy . . . and then we met.

o o o

My husband would never chase after another woman. He's too fine, too decent, too decrepit.

o o o

The years a woman subtracts from her age are not lost. They are added to the ages of other women.

o o o

Even back in the Stone Age, when women wrote down their ages, they were chiseling.

o o o

Why is a man more easily pacified than a woman? Because man was made out of soft earth, and woman out of a hard rib.

—Dosetai ben Yannai

o o o

His imbibing with bourbon on the rocks put his marriage on the skids.

o o o

He needs two women—a secretary to take everything down and a wife to pick everything up.

o o o

If the divorce rate keeps increasing, part of the marriage vow will have to be changed from "I do" to "adieu."

—Hy Gardner

o o o

A woman, trying on a fur coat, said to the salesgirl: "I wish it were called something besides broadtail. My husband thinks he is a comedian."

o o o

My wife makes a monkey out of herself just by carrying a tale.

o o o

Money isn't everything
There are greater things in life,
If only you can think of them

And then convince your wife!

° ° °

Do things together with your wife. If she wants to go for a walk, go for a walk with her. If she wants to go to the movies, go to the movies with her. And, most important, if she wants to mop the floor, mop the floor with her.

° ° °

A wife asked her husband, "Last year we got mother a chair. What do you think we ought to do for her this year?" The husband responded, "Electrify it."

° ° °

Marriage always demands the greatest understanding of the art of insincerity possible between two human beings.

—Vicki Baum (1888-1961)

° ° °

Some people go to a psychiatrist, others get married.

° ° °

Getting married is a good deal like going to a restaurant with your friends. You order what you want, and then when you see what the other fellow got, you wish you had taken that.

—Clarence Darrow

° ° °

"Don't you think marriage could be described as a lottery?" Clarence Darrow once was asked.

"Yes," he replied, "if only there were prizes."

° ° °

What marriage really needs is more open minds and a lot fewer open mouths.

° ° °

Getting a husband is like buying an old house. You don't see it the way it is, but the way you think it's going to be when you get it remodeled.

° ° °

Bride: A woman with a fine prospect of happiness behind her.

—Ambrose Bierce

° ° °

Bachelors know more about women than married men; if they didn't they'd be married too.

—H.L. Mencken

° ° °

Scratch a lover, and find a foe.

—Dorothy Parker

° ° °

A bachelor is a single man who has not nearly the value he would have in a state of union. He is an incomplete animal. He resembles the odd half of a pair of scissors.

—Benj. Franklin

° ° °

Lycoris has buried all her female friends, Fabianus. I wish she could make friends with my wife.

—*Martial*

° ° °

For dying or marrying there's always time.

° ° °

George Wallace has bigger eyes for women than ears.

—Barbara Howar, *Laughing All the Way*

° ° °

Romance: A Comedy of Eros.

° ° °

Alas! Another instance of the triumph of hope over experience.

—Samuel Johnson, commenting on the second marriage of a friend who had been unhappy with his first wife.

° ° °

Back of every achievement is a proud wife and a surprised mother-in-law.

—Ruth Graham

° ° °

I may be a five-ton truck at the office, but at home I'm nothing but a trailer.

° ° °

The gods gave man fire, and he invented the fire-engine; they gave him love and he invented marriage.

° ° °

Marriage: a ceremony in which rings are put on the finger of the lady and through the nose of the gentleman.

—Herbert Spencer

° ° °

My honeymoon is over. Now, my dog brings me my slippers and my wife barks.

° ° °

I should have married an archeologist; then the older I would get the more he would love me.

° ° °

The wife who always insists on the last word, often has it.

° ° °

The wife in curlpapers is replaced by the wife who puts on lipstick before she wakens her husband.

—Margaret Mead

° ° °

Here's to matrimony, the high sea for which no compass has yet been invented!

—Heine

° ° °

One wife is enough for any man.

—Ibn Ezra

° ° °

When I got married I must have said, "To love, to nourish, and to perspire.

° ° °

She falls in love with a fellow
Who swells with a foreign air;
He marries her for her money,
She marries him for his hair!
One of the very best matches—
Both are well mated in life;
She's got a fool for a husband,
He's got a fool for a wife.

° ° °

Marriage is like a railroad sign. When you see a pretty girl you stop. Then you look. After you're marked you listen.

° ° °

"I have five children," said the woman to the census taker, "four living and one married."

° ° °

My marriage was like a tourniquet; it stopped my circulation.

° ° °

When a man decides to get married, it may be the last decision he is allowed to make.

—Kenneth L. Krichbaum

° ° °

To my wife:
Better a bachelor's life
Than a slovenly wife.

° ° °

The man who marries to have someone to tell his troubles to soon has plenty to talk about.

° ° °

My wife has just one extravagance: she likes to spend money.

° ° °

Married men don't live longer than single men; it just seems longer.

° ° °

No, I've never thought of divorce; but murder, a thousand times.

° ° °

It isn't another mouth to feed that frightens me about marriage; it is another mouth to listen to.

° ° °

Arguing with my wife is like trying to blow out a neon light.

° ° °

Marriage is like a boxing card—the preliminaries are often much better than the main bout.

° ° °

To be married is to be one of the silent majority.

° ° °

Everybody has to be married sometime—you can't go through life just being happy.

° ° °

I'm not married; I just look this way because someone just stole my car.

° ° °

A lawyer wired one of his clients: "Your mother-in-law passed away in her sleep last night. Shall we order burial, embalming, or cremation?" The client wired back, "Take no chances, order all three."

° ° °

My wedding ceremony lasted for an hour, but my troubles will last for a lifetime.

° ° °

Wife: "You don't bring me candy any more, as you did before we were married."

Husband: "Did you ever see anyone continue to feed worms to a fish after it is caught?"

° ° °

I was a widow when I married my husband and if he wants to be separated I want him to leave me the way I was before.

° ° °

My husband is like the sun, just as the sun disappears every evening, so does he.

° ° °

I have a dog that growls, a fireplace that smokes, a parrot that curses and a cat that stays out all night. So tell me, what did I need my husband for?

• • •

Wives are like fisherman; they complain about the one they caught, and brag about the one that got away.

• • •

My wife divorced me because of illness. She got sick of me.

• • •

My breakfast consists of a three-minute boiled egg and a five-minute argument.

• • •

There was an actress who got rid of 215 pounds of excessively flabby fat in 90 days. She divorced him.

• • •

My wife lost her head and ran out of the house Wednesday night—but then I lost mine and let her back in.

• • •

My wife has everything a man can desire—including muscles and a moustache.

• • •

Love: a temporary insanity curable by marriage.

—Ambrose Bierce

• • •

If they can make penicillin out of moldy bread—they can make something out of my husband.

• • •

If I sued my husband for divorce, I'd name his mirror as correspondent.

• • •

That Jackie-Ari marriage is O.K.—apparently some of those old Greek ruins still work.

• • •

My wife is such a lousy cook that in our house we have Alka Seltzer on tap.

• • •

My wife follows a cookbook which comes with 200 assorted get-well cards.

• • •

Being asked whether it was better to marry or not, he (Socrates) replied, "Whichever you do you will repent it."

—Diogenes Laertius (Socrates)

• • •

Nobody introduced me to my wife. We just happened to

meet. I'm not blaming anybody.

° ° °

Marriages are made in Heaven—but so are thunder and lightning.

° ° °

The reason I don't perform marriages is because marriages aren't considered federal offenses.

—Justice Felix Frankfurter

° ° °

Music played at weddings always reminds me of the music played for soldiers before they go off to battle.

—Heinrich Heine (1797-1856)

° ° °

He's a confirmed bachelor who thinks that the only thoroughly justified marriage was the one that produced him.

—Harlan Miller

° ° °

When he told her this was going to be a battle of wits, she replied, "How brave of you to fight unarmed."

° ° °

Beneath this stone my wife doth lie:
Now she's at rest, and so am I!

—Boileau

° ° °

Here lies my poor wife, without bed or blanket,
But dead as a door-nail, and God be thankit.

° ° °

Oh, how many torments lie in the small circle of a wedding ring!

—Colley Cibber

° ° °

I remember when I got married. I remember where I got married. For the life of me, I can't remember why I got married.

° ° °

"My wife is an angel."
"Lucky for you. Mine is still living."

° ° °

When you're away, my loving wife
I'm lonely, bored, dejected,
But here's the rub my darling dear
I feel the same when you are here!

° ° °

A husband is a person who is under the impression he bosses

the house when in reality, he only houses the boss.

° ° °

My wife is dead, and here she lies,
Nobody laughs and nobody cries;
Where she is gone to and how she fares,
Nobody knows, and nobody cares.

—On a tombstone

° ° °

She was the type of wife who wore the pants so frequently that she found the other woman who was wearing the mink.

° ° °

America is the land of permanent waves and impermanent wives.

—Brendan Behan

° ° °

They were married for better or for worse. He couldn't have done better and she couldn't have done worse.

° ° °

Helmate—A wife, or bitter half.

° ° °

There is one thing more exasperating than a wife who can cook and won't, and that is the wife who can't cook and will.

° ° °

A man in love is incomplete until he has married. Then he's finished.

—Zsa Zsa Gabor in *Newsweek*

° ° °

When the husband is not a self-starter, the wife becomes a crank.

° ° °

I'm not saying she's a bad cook, but I know now why her family prays before every meal.

° ° °

I bequeath all my property to my wife on the condition that she remarry immediately. Then there will be at least one man to regret my death.

—Heinrich Heine

° ° °

Taking a stroll with my wife is like walking with a Walkie-Talkie.

° ° °

I've been married so long that I almost feel I was born in captivity.

° ° °

Keeping a secret from my wife is like trying to smuggle daylight past a rooster.

° ° °

My wife is an expert at serving cold shoulder and hot tongue.

° ° °

You say you are henpecked, but the real trouble is that you come home with nothing but chicken feed.

° ° °

My wife called me from Jerusalem last night. It was wonderful to hear her voice, knowing that she is over six thousand miles away.

° ° °

My wife may be a vision at dinner, but she's a sight at breakfast.

° ° °

Wedlock is a padlock.

—John Ray

° ° °

The oyster is not the only one who has a crab for a mate.

° ° °

June is the month of weddings and cooking. The billing follows.

° ° °

THE PROFESSIONALS
INTRODUCTION

The most satisfying kind of target practice is to aim at those professionals who think they are God's gift to the human race: to doctors who strut around as though they had all the answers; to attorneys who thrive on their particular type of mumbo jumbo, and to professionals who take themselves too seriously.

How you would like to bring them down a peg or two! How would you like to call your lawyer a liar, or your doctor a quack, or your psychiatrist a head shrinker, or your druggist a soda jerk?

Gagsters have made up complete categories of jokes and stories about professional men and women. They have been classified under medical humor, hospital humor, court humor, college humor, army humor, etc. . . And, of course, every trade and profession, from time to time, laughs at itself. It's good for business and healthy for the ego. Take the anonymous scientist who jabbed at relativity with these words:

> There was once a twin brother named Bright
> Who could travel much faster than light.
> He departed one day, in a relative way,
> And came home on the previous night.

Poking fun at doctors at least eases the pain of paying the bills. For example, "My doctor is one in a million. He put me on my feet in no time. Made me sell my car to pay his bill." It gets a laugh, and you think you are even with him. The doctor? He laughs all the way to the bank.

Or take the judge who took a crack at the legal profession this way: "You are lying so clumsily, I would advise you to get a lawyer."

Judges don't go unscathed either. Take the case of the Kentucky judge who suddenly thundered in his courtroom, "Silence in the court! Half a dozen men have been convicted already without the court's having been able to hear a word of the testimony." This hits where it hurts, and rightfully so. Which one of us hasn't, at one time or another, felt that the judge wasn't interested, or didn't hear because he wasn't listening?

The stress of life can be relieved if we can take pot shots at those who are out of reach. So we refer to a critic as a Pygmy with a poison dart who lives in the valley of sleeping giants. In reference to the diplomat we conclude that diplomacy is the verbal technique of saying what you don't mean and making it mean what you don't say. To add insult to injury, we add the following about diplomats: "A diplomat must learn three things: to speak French, to say nothing, and to tell lies." It does help to relieve the tension. Art Buchward, American journalist and essayist offered this one about generals: "Old soldiers never die—they just write their memoirs."

George Bernard Shaw was an expert at the verbal dart, the poisoned arrow. "Tyrants of genius are succeeded by scoundrels." Jacob Epstein, the famous sculptor had this to say about his profession: "The successful portrait sculptor needs a front of brass, the hide of a rhinoceros, and all the guile of a courtier."

Henry Ward Beecher, speaking out against honorary degrees, once said, "If any college should put two D's after his name he should feel inclined to put a dash between them and send them back."

A fast comeback is an asset to the speaker. For example, when Garrick was invited by a nobleman to be a candidate for Parliament, the actor answered, "No, my lord. I would rather play the part of a great man on the stage, than the part of a fool in Parliament."

And so here you have the next portion of the book. Read the quips and remember them. You never know when you'll be called upon to say a few words—to introduce a doctor, a judge, or a dentist. Then, if you use your head, you might just become the funniest man in town. If your rehearsed gags fall short, blame it on this collector. After all, aren't we finding fault with professionals?

THE PROFESSIONALS

No priest's dress is so tight that the Devil can't be buttoned up in it.

—Russian Proverb

o o o

The devil is not so dangerous when he comes as a roaring lion as when he comes as a wagging dog.

o o o

History is something that never happened, written by a man who wasn't there.

o o o

History is bunk.

—Henry Ford 1863-1947

o o o

A lecturer is one with his hand in your pocket, his tongue in your ear, and his faith in your patience.

—Ambrose Bierce

o o o

There is a lot of history that isn't fit to repeat itself.

—F.D. Roosevelt

o o o

The instability of the economy is equaled only by the instability of economists.

—John W. Williams

o o o

A toastmaster is a man who eats a meal he doesn't want so he can get up and tell a lot of stories he doesn't remember to people who have already heard them.

—George Jessel

o o o

A Harvard professor is an educator who thinks the American eagle has two left wings.

—Rep. John M. Ashbrook (R. Ohio)

o o o

Teaching is the last refuge of feeble minds with classical education.

—Huxley

o o o

Some college graduates I know ought to carry their diplomas with them to prove they've been to college.

—Prof. Israel J. Kapstein

o o o

Arrogance, pedantry, and dogmatism are the occupational diseases of those who spend their lives directing the intellects of the young.

—Henry Canby

o o o

Nothing in education is so astonishing as the amount of ignorance it accumulates in the form of inert facts.

—Henry Brooks Adams

o o o

Dumping a little of everything into the school makes of education intellectual garbage.

—E.D. Martin

o o o

Colleges don't make fools; they only develop them.

—George Horace Lorimer

o o o

The college campus today is one of our biggest supporters of wild life.

—Dana Robbins

o o o

The reason social scientists are less dependable than the weather man in their prognosis is that they know even less about the mental climate than he does about the weather.

o o o

The most solemn promise of a statesman is a definite maybe.

o o o

If speakers had the habit of clearing their minds as well as their throats before they speak, they would speak less and say more.

o o o

Instead of putting so much fire into their speeches, some lecturers ought to put more speeches into the fire.

o o o

As a diplomat his political and economic slogans are mouth-filling but mind-emptying.

o o o

With pen and pencil we're learning to say
Nothing more cleverly, every day.

—William Alingham

o o o

'Tis a vanity common to all writers, to over-value their own productions.

—Dryden

o o o

Critics! Appalled, I venture on the name,
Those cut-throat bandits in the paths of fame.

—Robert Burns

o o o

Diplomacy is the art of saying things in such a way that nobody knows exactly what you mean.

o o o

Once, while William Howard Taft was making a speech, he was constantly being interrupted by heckling from the gallery. Finally, a cabbage landed on the stage, near his feet. Pausing in his speech, Taft announced, "Ladies and Gentlemen, I see that one of my adversaries has lost his head."

o o o

As a speaker, he does not electrify his audience; he merely gasses them.

o o o

Hypocrisy is the occupational disease of a diplomat.

° ° °

And Nathan, being sick, trusted not in the Lord, but sent for a physician—and Nathan was gathered unto his fathers.

—The Bible

° ° °

You are now a gladiator; you were formerly an occulist. You did as an ophtalmic surgeon what you now do as a gladiator.

—*Martial.*

° ° °

This house where once a lawyer dwelt,
Is now a smith's. Alas!
How rapidly the iron age
Succeeds the age of brass!

—Erskine

° ° °

"Virtue in the middle," said the Devil, as he seated himself between two lawyers.

° ° °

God heals, and the doctor takes the fee.

—Benjamin Franklin, *Poor Richard*

° ° °

Lawyer's houses are built on the heads of fools.

—George Herbert

° ° °

Necessity knows no law; I know some attorneys of the same.

—Benjamin Branklin, *Poor Richart*

° ° °

Doctors make the worst patients.

—Proverb

° ° °

That patient is not like to recover, who makes the doctor his heir.

—Proverb

° ° °

A good many young writers make the mistake of enclosing a stamped, self-addressed envelope, big enough for the manuscript to come back in. This is too much of a temptation to the editor.

—Ring Lardner

° ° °

They lard their lean books with the fat of others' works.

—Robert Burton, *Anatomy of Melancholy*

∘ ∘ •

In comparing various authors with one another, I have discovered that some of the gravest and latest writers have transcribed, word for word, from former works, without making acknowledgment.

—Pliny the Elder, *Natural History*

∘ ∘ ∘

Of late, even two beer cans on a wooden tray have been classified as sculpture.

∘ ∘ •

Art: Man's feeble effort to imitate the Lord. Looking at certain canvasses, I wonder if the Lord is flattered.

∘ ∘ ∘

The clergy spends too much time in the vestry and too little time in the street.

• ∘ ∘

Book Reviewing: A profession in which those who flunked the course get to teach the class.

• ∘ ∘

Biographies are rarely worth reading being written by antagonists or flatterers.

• ∘ •

We now live in the Era of Incompetence; we have painters who can't paint, poets who can't rhyme and composers who whistle dissonance.

—Dagobert D. Runes

∘ ∘ ∘

"I want to apologize for dozing just a little during your fine sermon," said the lady to the minister. "But," she concluded, "I want you to know I didn't miss a thing."

∘ ∘ ∘

"You'll never know what your sermon meant to me," said the woman to her minister. "Why, it was just like water to a drowning man."

∘ • ∘

What a blessed thing it is that nature, when she invented, manufactured, and patented her authors, contrived to make critics out of the chips that were left!

—Holmes

∘ ∘ •

Loud-bawling orators were driven by their weakness to noise, as lame men to take horse.

—Cicero

∘ • ∘

A historian is an unsuccessful novelist.

—H.L. Mencken

° ° °

The only time he got ten dollars a word is when he talked back to the judge.

—About an author

° ° °

There is probably no hell for authors in the next world—they suffer so much from critics and publishers in this.

—Christian Bovee

° ° °

The maid asked for an advance on her salary, saying, "Our preacher is leaving the church this Sunday and the congregation wants to give him a little momentum."

° ° °

He was the kind of a doctor who diagnosed your ailment by feeling your purse.

° ° °

When the physician said, "Sir, you are an old man," Pausania answered, "because you never were my doctor."

—Plutarch

° ° °

A Chinese describes a trial in the English law courts as follows: "One man is quite silent, another talks all the time, and then twelve men condemn the man who never said a word."

° ° °

Statisticians collect facts and draw their own confusions.

° ° °

"This is the finest collection of frames I've ever seen," said Sir Humphry Davy when he returned from a visit to a Paris art gallery.

° ° °

"He's not the kind of doctor that does anybody any good," said the maid of the great physicist, Robert A. Millikan, to a telephone caller.

° ° °

A painter was advised to turn physician: for now all his faults were seen; then they would be buried.

° ° °

The professor was interrupted by the sound of the bell and was annoyed to see the hasty exit of his students. "Just a moment, gentlemen," he said, "I have a few more pearls to cast."

° ° °

When he was told that Harvard University was one of the nation's greatest storehouses of knowledge, Charles W. Eliot, the president answered, "That's because we're adding more knowledge every semester. The freshmen bring us so much of it and the seniors take away so little!"

° ° °

A college education is a four-year plan for confusing a young mind methodically.

° ° °

The Devil is always dressed in the latest fashion.

° ° °

In regard to the fascinating subject of my operation, I should naturally like to go on for several pages . . . but will confine myself to saying that I think the doc should have read just one book before picking up the saw.

—Kennedy, writing to a friend after his operation in 1944

° ° °

My teacher, with all his unusual knowledge, acted like a woman with a fancy petticoat; he found it hard to forego the temptation to display some of it.

° ° °

Wanted: a smart, good-looking woman, to act as deceptionist.

° ° °

Pension: In England, understood to mean pay given to a state hireling for treason to his country.

—Dr. Samuel Johnson

° ° °

Doctors think a lot of patients are cured who have simply quit in disgust.

—Don Herold

° ° °

The trouble with the publishing business is that too many people who have half a mind to write a book do so.

° ° °

Lawyer: One skilled in circumvention of the law.

—Ambrose Bierce

° ° °

Liar: A lawyer with a roving commission.

—Ambrose Bierce

° ° °

History: An account mostly false, of events mostly unimportant, which are brought about by rulers mostly knaves, and soldiers mostly fools.

—Ambrose Bierce

° ° °

Actors are a nuisance in the earth, the very offal of society.

—Timothy Dwight

° ° °

I always thought he was a crummy actor but Tony Randall is versatile—he's crummy at a lot of things.

—"Roaster"

° ° °

He's the kind of a man that gets up a reputation for being clever and artistic by running down the very one particular thing that everyone likes . . . some book or picture or play that no one has ever heard of.

—Frank Norris, *The Pit*

° ° °

A countryman between lawyers is like a fish between two cats.

—Benjamin Franklin

° ° °

Fond of doctors, little health,
Fond of lawyers, little wealth.

° ° °

Journalism is organized gossip.

—Edward Eggleston

° ° °

God sends meat, the devil sends cooks.

—Charles VI

° ° °

Double Jeopardy—When your doctor calls in a consulting physician.

° ° °

The best doctor is the one you run for and can't find.

—Diderot

° ° °

Till lately Dialus was a doctor; now he is an undertaker. What he does as an undertaker, he had learned already as a doctor.

—*Martial*

° ° °

The alienist is not a joke:
He finds you cracked, and leaves you broke.

—Keith Preston

° ° °

He became mellow before he became ripe.

—Alexander Woolcott, about Christopher Morley

° ° °

You can gain nothing by reading her. It is like eating snowballs, with which one can surfeit one's self without satisfying the stomach.

—Napoleon Bonaparte

° ° °

Mr. Henry James writes fiction as if it were a painful duty.

—Oscar Wilde

° ° °

Publishing a column of verse is like dropping a rose petal down the Grand Canyon and waiting for the echo.

—Don Marquis

° ° °

On the performance of a famous violinist: "Difficult do you call it, sir? I wish it were impossible."

—Samuel Johnson

° ° °

I wish I was as cocksure of anything as Tom Macaulay is of everything.

—William Lamb Melbourne

° ° °

He may be witty, but he who wrote *Snow Bound* was Whittier.

° ° °

Play Hemingway. Be fierce.

—Gertrude Stein, to her dog.

° ° °

Alfred Lunthas his head in the clouds and his feet in the box office.

—Noel Coward

° ° °

Never did I see such apparatus get ready for thinking, and so little thought. He mounts scaffolding, pulleys, and tackles, gathers all the tools in the neighborhood with labour, with noise, demonstration, precept, and sets—three bricks.

—Thomas Carlyle, about Samuel T. Coleridge

° ° °

I have no wish to know anyone sitting in a sewer and adding to it.

—Thomas Carlyle, on refusing to meet Algernon Swinburne

° ° °

There are two ways of disliking poetry, one way is to dislike it, the other is to read Pope.

—Oscar Wilde

° ° °

Bernard Shaw had discovered himself and gave ungrudgingly of his discovery to the world.

—Saki

° ° °

M. Zola is determined to show that, if he has not got genius, he can at least be dull.

—Oscar Wilde

° ° °

The first rule for a young playwright to follow is not to write like Henry Arthur Jones. The second and third rules are the same.

—Oscar Wilde

° ° °

An empty cab drove up and Sarah Bernhardt got out.

—Arthur Bugs Baer

° ° °

If its length be not considered a merit, it hath no other.

—Edmund Waller, about *Paradise Lost*

° ° °

Wagner's music is better than it sounds.

—Mark Twain

° ° °

Tennyson is a beautiful half of a poet.

—Ralph Waldo Emerson

° ° °

Why was I born with such contemporaries?

—George Bernard Shaw

° ° °

He leads his readers to the latrine and locks them in.

—Oscar Wilde, about George Moore

° ° °

On the comparitive talents of the poets Samuel Derrick and Christopher Smart: "Sir, there is no setting the point of precedency between a louse and a flea."

—Samuel Johnson

° ° °

He had written much blank verse, and blanker prose,
And more of both than anybody knows.

—George Gordon, about Robert Southey

° ° °

Hemingway remarks are not literature.

—Gertrude Stein

° ° °

He has no vision in him. He will neither see nor do any great thing, but be a poor Holland House unbeliever, with spectacles instead of eyes, to the end of him.

—Thomas Carlyle, about Thomas Macauley

° ° °

"Did you ever hear me preach?" asked Samuel T. Coleridge.

"I never heard you do anything else," answered Charles Lamb.

° ° °

George Moore, brilliant English until he discovered grammar.

—Oscar Wilde

° ° °

The same old sausage, fizzing and sputtering in its own grease.

—Henry James, about Thomas Carlyle

° ° °

Shakespeare never has six lines together without a fault.

—Samuel Johnson

° ° °

A musician, of more ambition than talent, composed an elegy at the death of composer Edward MacDowell. She played the elegy for the pianist Josef Hoffman, then asked his opinion. "Well, it's quite nice," he replied. "But don't you think it would have been better if you had died and MacDowell had written the elegy?"

° ° °

A day away from Tallaluah is like a month in the country.

° ° °

Playwright Ferenc Molnar solved the problem of unwelcome callers by instructing his secretary to say, "Sorry, he's not in. He left a moment ago, and if you rush down the street you'll catch him."

° ° °

Dr. Alfred Adler, psychiatrist, was lecturing on the theory that people tend to emphasize their handicaps in their work. Thus, fat boys tend to become long-distance runners, people with bad eyes become painters, stutterers become actors, and so forth. When he asked for questions,one young man asked, "Dr. Adler, wouldn't your theory show that weak-minded people tend to become psychiatrists?"

° ° °

Mr. James Payn is adept in the art of concealing what is not worth finding.

—Oscar Wilde

° ° °

"Trees" is one of the most annoying pieces of verse within my knowledge. Surely the Kilmer tongue must not have been very far from the Kilmer cheek when he wrote, "Poems are made by fools like me."

—Heywood Broun

° ° °

Shakespeare boasted that as a country schoolmaster he had never blotted out a line. I wish he'd blotted out a thousand.

—Dr. Johnson

° ° °

As a career, the business of an orthodox preacher is about as successful as that of a celluloid dog chasing an asbestos cat through hell.

—Elbert Hubbard

° ° °

Doctors is all swabis.

—Robert L. Stevenson, *Treasure Island*

° ° °

A psychiatrist is a fellow who convinces you that your parents were failures because you turned out to be a louse.

° ° °

Witch doctors are as important as psychiatrists.

—Dr. T. Adeoye Lambe

° ° °

If experience is the best teacher, the whole faculty should be fired.

—Franklin P. Jones

° ° °

No wonder they wear masks in the operating room!

—Patient receiving bill for operation

° ° °

The only thing wrong with architecture is the architects.

—Frank Lloyd Wright

° ° °

Scientists say we are what we eat. Nuts must be a commoner diet than we had thought.

° ° °

My doctor is so stingy that when I complained of loss of

memory he made me pay in advance.

° ° °

I have two sons. One is in politics and the other isn't much good either.

° ° °

He plays Abraham Lincoln so many times, he won't be satisfied until he is assassinated.

° ° °

My psychiatrist is so expensive that for $25 all he does is send you a get-well card.

° ° °

Anyone who goes to a psychiatrist ought to have his head examined.

° ° °

The best of doctors are destined for hell.

° ° °

It was difficult for the Angel of Death to kill everybody in the whole world, so he appointed doctors to assist him.

—Nahman Bratzlav

° ° °

Both the doctor and the Angel of Death kill, but the former charges a fee.

° ° °

George Gershwin played good tennis almost by ear.

—Oscar Levant

° ° °

Our doctor is dead; ah well, dry your tears;
Death's sad, but what use to resent it?
For, if he had lived another few years,
There'd be none of us here to lament it.

° ° °

Johnny Carson is a comedian who is seen every night in millions of bedrooms all over America . . . and that's why his last wife left him. She found out he gave a better performance in those bedrooms than he did in his own.

—A comedian at a roaster

° ° °

Joe has a great respect for girls. Only last week in New York, he saved a girl from being attacked. He controlled himself.

—Dean Martin, about Joe Namath

° ° °

Emily Kimbrough was about to begin her lecture, when a workman appeared on the stage. A minute later, the chairlady rose and announced, "I'm sorry to say there will be a slight delay. Word has just been given me that there is a screw loose in our speaker."

o o o

Bats feel proud in the absence of birds.

o o o

"You are lying so clumsily," said the judge, "that I advise you to get a lawyer."

o o o

A celebrated lawyer once said that the three most troublesome clients he ever had were a young lady who wanted to be married, a married woman who wanted a divorce, and an old maid who didn't know what she wanted.

o o o

The young lawyer was trying to impress the jury with the magnitude of the injury. "Imagine the loss," he said, "twenty-four hogs were killed. Twenty four! Twice the number there are in the jury box."

o o o

An English lawyer being sick, made his last will, and gave all his estate to fools and madmen. Being asked the reason for so doing: "From such," said he, "I had it, and to such I give it again."

o o o

As an actor, he thought he was elevating the stage when in reality he was depressing the audience.

o o o

If all the world's economists were laid end to end—they wouldn't even reach a conclusion.

—George Bernard Shaw

o o o

I have hardly ever known a mathematician who was capable of reasoning.

—Pluto

o o o

Architect: One who drafts a plan of your house, and plans a draft of your money.

—Ambrose Bierce

o o o

A lawyer is a learned gentleman who rescues your estate from your enemies and keeps it himself.

—Lord Brougham

o o o

Doctors are men, who prescribe medicines of which they

know little, to cure diseases of which they know less, in human beings of whom they know nothing.

—Voltaire

° ° °

Plastic surgeons can do anything with a nose except keep it out of other people's business.

° ° °

Doctors and grave-diggers are partners.

° ° °

A banker is a man who lends you an umbrella when the weather is fair, and takes it away from you when it rains.

° ° °

There shoud be a check on doctors who graduated God knows when, who don't know what's new and don't care, and who get what information they get from Time, Life and the Reader's Digest.

—Dr. Louis N. Katz,
Chicago Heart Specialist

° ° °

Hollywood impresses me as being ten million dollars' worth of intricate and highly ingenious machinery functioning elaborately to put skin on baloney.

—George Jean Nathan

° ° °

Daniel Webster struck me much like a steam engine in trousers.

—Sydney Smith

° ° °

The first thing we do, let's kill all the lawyers.

—Shakespeare, *Henry VI*

° ° °

Actresses often paint, but they do not always draw.

—W.S. Gilbert

° ° °

They couldn't find the artist, so they hung his picture.

—From an art critic's column

° ° °

The trouble with opera in the United States is that it is trying to sell caviar to a hamburger-eating country.

—Helen Traubel, Opera Star

° ° °

A prating barber asked Archelaus how he would like to be trimmed. He answered, "In Silence."

—Plutarch

° ° °

A faculty member of a London medical college posted this notice in his classroom: "Professor Grimes wishes to inform his class that he has been appointed honorary physician to Her Majesty, Queen Elizabeth." When the professor came to his classroom in the afternoon, he found inscribed under this notice: God Save the Queen.

° ° °

In the old days an actress tried to become a star. Today we nave stars trying to be actresses.

—Sir Laurence Olivier

° ° °

As long as more people will pay admission to a theater to see a naked body than to see a naked brain, the drama will languish.

—George Bernard Shaw

° ° °

I am going from bad to Hearst.

—William L. Shirer

° ° °

In Hollywood the woods are full of people that learned to write, but evidently not to read. If they could read their stuff, they'd stop writing.

—Will Rogers

° ° °

Some of the greatest love affairs I've known have involved one actor—unassisted.

—Wilsom Maner

° ° °

Ever illustrating the obvious, explaing the evident—expatiating the commonplace.

—Benjamin Disraeli about a lawyer.

° ° °

When Somerset Maugham, the writer, was recuperating in London from the flu, he was phoned by a lady admirer, who asked if she might send fruit and flowers. Replied the 88-year-old Maugham: "It's too late for fruit—too early for flowers."

° ° °

"Tell me, George, if you had it to do all over again, would you fall in love with yourself again?"

—Oscar Levant to George Gershwin

° ° °

Oscar Wilde reached his climax, "And so you Philistines have invaded the sacred sanctum of art!"

"I suppose that's why we are being assaulted with the jawbone of an ass," cried a spectator.

• ◦ •

Diplomacy is to do and say
The nastiest thing in the nicest way.

◦ ◦ ◦

A diplomat is one who can cut his neighbor's throat without having his neighbor notice it.

—Trygve Lie

◦ ◦ ◦

An ambassador is an honest man sent abroad to lie for the commonwealth.

—Sir Henry Wotton

◦ • ◦

There are three species of creature who when they seem coming are going, when they are seen going they come: diplomats, women, and crabs.

—John Hay

◦ ◦ ◦

Speech was given to him so he could disguise his thoughts.

◦ ◦ ◦

When a reporter asked a diplomat an important question about an international problem, the diplomat snapped, "Don't bother me now. I must make a speech. This is no time to think."

—Walter Winchell

◦ ◦ ◦

I have discovered the art of fooling diplomats. I speak the truth and they never believe me.

—Benso di Vacour

◦ ◦ ◦

A diplomat is a person who can tell you to go to hell in such a way that you actually look forward to the trip.

—Caskie Stinnett—Out of the Red

◦ ◦ ◦

Modern diplomats approach every problem with an open mouth.

—Arthur J. Goldberg

◦ ◦ ◦

How can a diplomat smoke the peace pipe when he has his foot in his mouth?

◦ ◦ ◦

A diplomat is one who can tell a man he's open-minded when he means he has a hole in the head.

◦ • ◦

When a diplomat says yes he means perhaps; when he says perhaps he means no; when he says no, he is no diplomat.

o o o

Diplomacy: lying in state.

o o o

A diplomat is a peson who thinks twice before saying nothing.

o o o

The devil can recite Scripture for his purpose.

o o o

George Ade had finished his speech and seated himelf. A well-known lawyer rose, placed his hands into his trousers' pockets and laughingly asked, "Doesn't it strike you as a little unusual that a humorist should be funny?"

When the laughter subsided, Ade said, "Doesn't it strike you as a little odd that a lawyer should keep his hands in his own pockets?"

o o o

I have ceased to wonder at many things; but that two diplomats can look at each other without laughing, that still amazes me daily.

—Boerne

o o o

As the orchestra on the radio struck up a new tune, the daughter exclaimed,"Did you ever hear anything so perfectly stunning?"

"No," replied the father. "The nearest thing to it I ever heard was when a truck loaded with empty milk cans had a collision with another truck that was loaded with live ducks.

o o o

A lot of elocutionists can teach us how to speak, but none of them can teach us when.

o o o

Politician: "I am not prejudiced at all. I am going to this political convention with an open, unbiased mind, prepared to listen to a lot of pure tommyrot!"

o o o

CRITICS AND SPEECHMAKERS
Introduction

Are you an actor, writer, playwright, opera singer? Do you teach, sell, dance, make speeches? No matter what you do, there are mornings when your blood-pressure runs high and your appetite low, and where no matter the weather, the day looks dark and dismal.

Don't run to the clinic or phone your doctor! Don't subscribe to a series of medical tests! All you have is a case of "criticphobia," an epidemic that has more people on the ropes than any plague in all history. There are critics, some professional and some strictly amateur, who delight in finding fault. Some of us can live with the professional critic. After all, it's a way of earning a living, although as one old Greek scholar said, "It is a thing of no great difficulty to raise objections against another man's works, no, it is an easy matter. But to produce a better one in its place is a task extremely troublesome."

When you are in the line of fire, when you see that one of these self-styled experts is about to take a pot-shot at you, don't cringe or run. Instead, say to the world at large: "Is that so; says who?" When one of these "destroyers" says something—written or oral—that almost turns your ego into jello, or sends a chill down your spine, just say to yourself: "Oh, yeah!"

Ask yourself, "What is a critic?" A critic is a fault-finder who generally has as his aim destruction not construction. Criticizing gives him pleasure, builds his own ego, conceals from others (so he thinks) his own unproductive nature.

You ought to read what critics say about critics. Says one: "A critic is one who may know the way, but can't drive the car." Writes another: "A critic can tune a piano, but can't play a single note."

What you ought to do is to walk through public parks and take careful note of all the beautiful pieces of sculpture around. There are statues and statues, but did you ever find one erected in honor of a critic? Never! DOESN'T THIS TELL A STORY? Heed the words of Homer who wrote: "The man who acts the least, upbraids the most."

Remember that critics are just propagandists, and that your guess about your work is at least as good as anyone else's. Lowell, in A Fable for Critics, said:

Nature fits all her children with something to do,
He who would write and can't write, can surely review.

Yet, it must be admitted that some critics, though cruel, have been known to be witty. I like the Chinese proverb: "Those who have free seats at the play hiss first."

There are many things you might remember when you're being criticized. Think of the answer the needle gave to the sieve when it was criticized: "You have a big hole right through the middle." The needle replied, "Well, you must have a hundred yourself."

Be not afraid of the critic. Be not afraid of his humor. If he throws salt at you, you will not be harmed, unless you are raw.

Now, read on and enjoy!

CRITICS AND SPEECHMAKERS

My publisher is so crooked that every time I shake hands with him I count my fingers.

° ° °

An auctioneer is a man who proclaims with a hammer that he has picked a pocket with his tongue.

—Ambrose Bierce

° ° °

An historian is a broad-gauge gossip.

—Ambrose Bierce

° ° °

I was going to bring you a present but what do you give a man who has nothing?

—Jack Carter to Johnny Carson

° ° °

The show had two strikes against it—the seats faced the stage.

° ° °

For the first time in my life I envied my feet. They were asleep!

° ° °

All her high notes are promissory.

—Lydel Sims, criticism of a singer

° ° °

If words were invented to conceal thought, I think that newspapers are a great improvement on a bad invention.

—Henry David Thoreau

° ° °

A critic is one who knows the way but cannot drive the car.

° ° °

The cast was well balanced—they were all rotten.

° ° °

The actor did a one-man show and the critic wrote: "There were too many in the cast."

° ° °

"Wonderful sermon," she exclaimed. "Everything you said applies to somebody or other I know."

° ° °

Speakers do well to remember that in the reaction of the pew, a poor sermon is always regarded as too long.

° ° °

Opportunity has to knock, but in this case, all Temptation has to do is to stand outside and whistle.

° ° °

The priest had preached one of his most moving sermons on marriage—its beauty, its permanency, its love, its everlasting glory.

"It was a moving sermon," commented one parishioner.

"I wish I knew as little about the subject as he does," answered the other.

° ° °

During a pause in a long, tiring speech, one listener said to another, "What follows his talk?"

Replied the second listener, "Wednesday!"

° ° °

No need to be too grateful to the scientists for showing us how to get to the moon. After all, they're the ones who have almost made it necessary for us to evacuate the earth.

° ° °

She is flat a good deal of the time . . . She cannot sing with anything approaching professional finish . . . She communicates almost nothing of the music she presents.

—Paul Hume, about a concert given by Margaret Truman

° ° °

I have just read your lousy review buried in the back pages. You sound like a frustrated old man who never made a success, an eight-ulcer man on a four-ulcer job and all four ulcers working.

I never met you, but if I do you'll need a new nose and a supporter below. Westbrook Pegler, a guttersnipe, is a gentleman compared to you. You can take that as more of an insult that a reflection on your ancestry.

—Harry S. Truman, about Paul Hume

° ° °

Paul Hume didn't know a damn thing about music. Not a goddam thing. When he wrote about Margaret in the Washington Post, he showed he didn't know a thing about music. He was just a smart aleck and a showoff . . .

—Harry S. Truman, about Paul Hume

° ° °

That book is filled with a lot of bunk; I don't know what got into Daniels. He used to work for me when I was President, and he worked for Roosevelt, and I liked him. But when he wrote that book, he just seemed to go haywire in places.

—Harry S. Truman, about Jonathan Daniel's book, *The Man of Independence*

° ° °

Editor: "Did you make these up yourself?"
Writer: "Yep, out of my head."
Editor: "You must be."

° ° °

I have not wasted my life trifling with literary fools in taverns as Johnson did when he should have been been shaking England with the thunder of his spirit.

—G. Bernard Shaw

° ° °

A village of tasteless producers and scentless flowers, controlled by frightened little men armed with buckets of sand to extinguish any fires of creative originality that might break out.

—Art Cohen, about Hollywood

° ° °

Broadway is a place where people spend money they haven't earned to buy things they don't need to impress people they don't like.

—Walter Winchell

° ° °

Somebody once said that Joyce made the Liffey the Ganges of the literary world, but sometimes the smell of the Ganges of the literary world is not all that literary.

—Brendan Behan

° ° °

Let him be kept from paper, pen and ink
So may he cease to write, and learn to think.

—Matthew Prior

° ° °

To many people dramatic criticism must seem like an attempt to tatoo soap bubbles.

° ° °

Last night Mr. Chresto played King Lear at the Tabor Grand. All through the five acts of that Shakespearean tragedy he played the King as though under momentary apprehension that someone else was about to play the ace.

—Eugene Field

° ° °

Actor: "I'm a smash hit. Why, yesterday during the last act, I had the audience glued to their seats."

Critic: "Wonderful! Clever of you to think of it!"

° ° °

Tallulah Bankhead barged down the Nile last night as Cleopatra—and sank.

—John Mason Brown

° ° °

A would-be poet sent editor Eugene Field verse entitled, "Why Do I Live?" Field sent a rejection slip with this message: "Because you sent your poem by mail."

° ° °

Critic: A eunuch judging a man's lovemaking.
A skydreaming eagle without wings.
Pygmies with poison darts who live in
The valley of the sleeping giants.

—Dagobert D. Runes

° ° °

"If you want to see your name in print," saidd the editor to the budding writer, "print visiting cards."

° ° °

A Kansan was repeatedly reminded that his department store bill was "overdue in the amount of $00.00." At last he managed to pacify the computer—with a check for $00.00.

° ° °

Talking about a famous Hollywood producer who hasn't had a hit film in years, Ben Hecht commented, "He can compress the most words into the smallest ideas of any man I ever met."

° ° °

Oscar Wilde arrived at his club one evening, after witnessing a first production of a play that was a complete failure.

"Oscar, how did your play go tonight?" he was asked.

"The play was a success, but the audience was a failure," he replied.

° ° °

There is less in this than meets the eye.
—Tallulah Bankhead, after seeing a play by Maeterlinck

° ° °

Jack Benny played Mendolssohn last night. Mendelssohn lost.

—Told about Jack Benny

° ° °

When Mr. Wilbur calls his play HALFWAY TO HELL, he underestimates the distance.

—Brooks Atkinson

° ° °

Some of today's movies should be pitied rather than censored.

° ° °

Language may be a vehicle of thought, but in some cases and with some people it is just an empty wagon.

° ° °

"I expected to find Mr. Lloyd George a big man in every sense," said the chairman of the banquet, "but as you see he is small in stature."

Lloyd George rose and remarked, "In North Wales we measure a man from his chin up. You evidently measure from his chin down."

° ° °

One of Disraeli's admirers, speaking about him to John Bright, commented: "You should give him credit for what he accomplished, as he is a self-made man."

"I know he is," retorted Mr. Bright, "and he adores his maker."

° ° °

Someone once introduced Ed Wynn to the hostess. "This is Ed Wynn, who's not such a fool as he looks."

"That's right," replied the comedian. "That's the great difference between me and my friend."

° ° °

"I never talk about things when I don't know the facts," commented the egotistical scholar.

"That must limit your conversation frightfully," replied the lecturer.

° ° °

Beatrice Lillie was wearing an expensive pearl necklace. "What lovely pearls, Beatrice," commented a malicious woman, "are they real?"

Miss Lillie nodded.

"Of course you can always tell by biting them," said the cat. "Here, let me see."

"Gladly," said Miss Lillie, "but remember you can't tell real pearls with false teeth."

° ° °

Dear Mr. Churchill,

Thank you for the copy of your speeches lately delivered in the House of Commons. I shall lose no time in reading them."

—Liberal Member in the House of Commons

° ° °

A vegetarian met her friend one day, and noting the kid gloves on her friend's hand remarked, "Skin of a beast!"

"Why, what do you wear?" the friend asked.

"Silk," was the immediate reply.

"Entrails of a worm!" said the friend to the vegetarian.

° ° °

When someone called Will Rogers' attention to his ungrammatical use of the word "ain't," he replied: "Maybe ain't' ain't correct, but I notice that a lot of folks who ain't usin' ain't' ain't eatin'."

° ° °

A woman bounced into an art gallery and made a superficial tour of the exhibits. "Are these the masterpieces I have heard so much about?" she asked with some scorn, "I do not see anything in them."

Quietly, the curator said, "Madam, don't you wish you could?"

° ° °

Talking about a mutual acquaintance, a friend said to Voltaire, "It is good of you to say such pleasant things of him when he says such spiteful ones of you."

"Perhaps," replied Voltaire, "we are both mistaken."

° ° °

Heywood Broun was a careless dresser and did not pay too careful attention to his personal appearance. Once, when, he together with other correspondents was presented to General Pershing, the General eyed Broun and commented, "Have you fallen down, Mr. Broun?"

° ° °

Receiving an invitation to lunch with Lady Randolph, George Bernard Shaw wired: "Certainly not; what have I done to provoke such an attack on my well known habits?"

Lady Randolph wired back: "Know nothing of your habits;

hope they are not as bad as your manners."

o o o

These are fine novels of yours; they are invaluable to me. When I come home tired and take up one of them, I fall asleep directly.

—Comment of a faithful servant of Sir Walter Scott

o o o

Lincoln was told about a profound historian. "It may be doubted whether any man of our generation has plunged more deeply into the sacred fount of learning."

"Yes," commented Lincoln, "or come up drier."

o o o

PERFECTLY SCANDALOUS was one of those plays in which all of the actors unfortunately enunciated very clearly.

—Robert Benchley

o o o

The "House Beautiful" is the play lousy.

—Dorothy Parker

o o o

Its impact was like the banging together of two dish-cloths.

—Review of a play

o o o

The audience was swell. They were so polite, they covered their mouths when they yawned.

—Bob Hope

o o o

I walked out infuriated after the first act. The lyrics are just laundry lists.

—Leonard Bernstein, comment about a musical

o o o

This should be modified to the point of deletion.

—Editor's statement on a submitted manuscript

o o o

I saw the play under adverse conditions—the curtain was up.

—Groucho Marx

o o o

A pin has as much head as some authors, and a good deal more point.

—G.D. Prentice

o o o

If the celebrated playwright wasn't pickled he gave the best imitation of rambling alcoholism you ever saw.

—*Daily News* about Brendan Behan

o o o

"Is this pig?" asked the would-be-wit, holding his fork with a piece of meat on it.

To which end of the fork do you refer?" asked one of the fellow guests.

o o o

"I never go to church," boasted a lord to his Bishop.

"Why not?" inquired the Bishop.

"The reason I don't go is that there are so many hypocrites there."

"Don't let that stop you," said the Bishop. "There is always room for one more."

o o o

When it was remarked that Fouche, an associate of Talleyrand under Napoleon, had a profound contempt for human nature, Talleyrand replied, "To be sure; he has made a careful study of himself."

o o o

Brief review of a new book: "The covers are too far apart."

o o o

Brendan came over 100 proof. It wasn't an Act of God, but an act of Guinness.

—Jackie Gleason about Brendan Behan

o o o

He writes his plays for the ages—the ages between four and twelve.

—George Jean Nathan, *Play Review*

o o o

The scenery was beautiful but the actors got in front of it.

—Alexander Woolcott, *Play Review*

o o o

There is no such thing as a dirty theme—there are only dirty writers.

—George Jean Nathan

o o o

An editor is one who separates the wheat from the chaff and prints the chaff.

—Adlai Stevenson

o o o

Action is therefore the lowest of the arts, if it is an art at all.

—George F. Moore

o o o

Critics in general are venemous serpents that delight in hissing.

—W.B. Daniel

° ° °

You've wasted enough of our time with your junk. Why don't you go back to filling teeth? You can't write, you never could write, and you never will be able to write.

—A publisher to Zane Grey, about a novel which later sold 1,000,000 copies

° ° °

The only thing he ever wrote that was accepted by a magazine was a check for a year's subscription.

° ° °

A critic is a wet blanket that soaks everything it touches.

° ° °

I am systematically ignored by colleagues and periodically annihilated by some hack.

—Sigmund Freud, letter to Jung

° ° °

I have found the most divine sleeping pill—television.

—Eva Gabor

° ° °

Every fool can find faults that a great many wise men can't remedy.

—Proverb

° ° °

The critic leaves at curtain fall
To find, in starting to review it,
He scarcely saw the play at all
For watching his reaction to it.

° ° °

Obscenity is whatever happens to shock elderly and ignorant magistrates.

—Bertrand Russell, *Look*, 2/23/54

° ° °

Reviewers are usually people who would have been poets, historians, biographers, if they could: they have tried their talents at one or the other, and have failed; therefore turn critics.

—S.T. Coleridge

° ° °

She runs the gamut of emotions from A to B.

—Dorothy Parker, of Hepburn's acting in "The Lake"

° ° °

Visiting Hollywood a few years before his death, French playwright Henri Bernstein was heard to observe:

Genius—geniuses everywhere I turn!
If there was only some talent!

° ° °

An author once asked an unhappy reader, "Have you read my last book?" The answer stunned him: "I hope so!"

° ° °

Sir Lewis Morris was complaining to Oscar Wilde about the neglect of his poems by the press.

"It is a complete conspiracy of silence against me," said Morris, "a conspiracy of silence. What do you suggest I do, Oscar?"

"Join it," said Wilde without hesitation.

° ° °

When Thomas Mann was visiting America, a Hollywood writer kept abasing himself before the novelist, emphasizing that he was nothing, a mere hack. Mann listened and then said to his host: "That man has no right to make himself so small. He is not that big."

° ° °

A critic is a legless man who teaches running.

—Channing Pollack

° ° °

Abraham Lincoln once wrote a review of a book with these words, "For those who like this kind of book, this is the kind of a book they will like."

° ° °

Rep. Ross Bass (D-Tenn) played it safe with the following Chinese scroll he hung on his office wall: *No Talkee, No Tellee, No Catchee Helee.*

° ° °

As a toastmaster he was living proof that not all oil cans are in the toolbox.

° ° °

How true it is about the speaker, who about to make a speech said: "Before I start my speech I'd like to say something."

° ° °

If all toastmasters were laid end to end across the country, it would be a good thing.

—George Jessel

° ° °

"Ladies and gentlemen, I am not going to bore you with a speech today, but I will present to you a man who will."

—Chairman, introducing a speaker

° ° °

His speeches are like the horns on a steer—a point here, a point there, and a lot of bull in between.

° ° °

Censorship: An idea fostered by people who want to stick their no's into everyone's business.

—Joan I. Welsh

° ° °

He can crowd more words into the smallest idea than any man I ever knew.

—Abraham Lincoln

° ° °

Lecture: Something that can make you feel numb at one end and dumb at the other.

° ° °

His long speech had only one redeeming feature—that it was mostly inaudible.

° ° °

When a speaker turned to the Sunday School class he was about to address and asked, "What would you want me to do?" they replied in chorus, "Keep quiet!"

° ° °

The coffee's cold, the sherbert wanes,
The speech drones on and on . . .
O, speaker, heed the ancient rule:
Be brief, be gay. Be gone!

° ° °

When asked how his speech was received, the speaker replied, "Terrible. It sounded like a caterpillar in sneakers romping across a Persian rug."

° ° °

He expresses himself much better when he is on his seat than on his feet.

° ° °

A government official received this invitation to speak at a Memorial Day celebration: You are invited to be one of the speakers at our Memorial Day services. The program will include a talk by the mayor, a recitation by a student, your talk, and then the firing squad.

° ° °

Too many speak who should be listening; too many write who should be reading.

° ° °

His speech was too long because he was selling the harvest

before he separated the wheat from the chaff.

o o o

I'm not going to begin my speech with Ladies and Gentlemen. I know you too well for that.

o o o

He is the kind of speaker who makes deep sounds from the chest seem like important messages from the brain.

o o o

Harry Hershfield, a great toastmaster, once started the evening with the usual "Ladies & Gentlemen." Someone yelled, "Louder!" Harry, looking right at the heckler, said, "You didn't miss anything. I said Ladies & Gentlemen."

o o o

He was the type of speaker who needed no introduction, just a conclusion.

o o o

He is a well known lecturer. In fact, he takes an annual boast to boast tour.

o o o

The English (it must be owned) are rather a foul-mouthed nation.

—William Hazlitte, Table Talk

o o o

Dolphins are smart enough to know they have nothing to gain by conversation with man.

—Roger Conklin of the Miami Seaquarium

o o o

Speaking about two men, Sidney Smith, celebrated wit, said, "There is the same difference between their tongues as between the hour and the minute hand on a clock. The one goes twelve times as fast, the other signifies twelves times as much.

o o o

Disraeli saw a deaf member of Parliament listening to the debate with the aid of an ear trumpet. "What a wanton waste," Disraeli exclaimed, "of the mercies of God's providence."

o o o

My grandaunt died in a state of acute indignation brought on by someone letting her hear Churchill's speech at the end of the war.

o o o

He was a proficient toastmaster who was so dull he made all the other speakers interesting.

o o o

His speeches to an hour-glass
Do some resemblance show;
Because the longer time they run
The shallower they grow.

° ° °

Why do you wrap up your neck in a woolen muffler when you are going to recite? The muffler would be more suitable for our ears.

—Martial

° ° °

Gentlemen, you have just been listening to that Chinese sage, On Too Long.

—Will Rogers

° ° °

The art of conversation has been murdered by lunatics, mostly from the United States.

—Brendan Behan

° ° °

After-Dinner speaking: An occupation monopolized by men; women can't wait that long.

° ° °

Stevenson makes the speeches and Estes Kefauver goes around the country explaining them.

—Republican comment about the Stevenson-Kefauver ticket

° ° °

A speech that's full of sparkling wit
Will keep its hearers grinning,
Provided that the end of it
Is close to the beginning!

° ° °

The toastmaster is the man at a dinner party whose duty it is to inform you that the best part of the evening is over.

° ° °

It was getting very close to the time for the celebrated guest to make his speech. The chairman, looking about the table, came over to the speaker and whispered, "Shall we let them enjoy themselves a little longer, or do you think you'd better begin your speech now?"

° ° °

Whatever I said in anger, whatever I shouted in spite, I'm sorry I spoke so quickly, I thought up some worse ones tonight!

° ° °

"What you are thunders so loud, I can't hear what you say.

The counterfeit coin looks like the genuine, but it is not. It won't bounce."

—Emerson

° ° °

Once, when introducing Thomas A. Edison at a dinner, the toastmaster mentioned his many inventions, dwelling at length on the talking machine. The aged inventor then rose to his feet, smiled, and said gently: "I thank the gentleman for his kind remarks, but I must insist upon a correction. God invented the talking machine. I only invented one that can be shut off."

° ° °

"Sir, you are like a pin, but without either its head or its point."

—Douglas Jerold to a speaker who was boring

° ° °

He was a great orator and was finishing his fiery oration with: "You cannot keep me down; though I may be pressed below the waves I rise again; you will find that I come to the surface, gentlemen."

Whereupon an old whaler in the audience shouted, "Yes, you come to the surface to blow."

° ° °

"I have to be on fire," thundered the reverend, "for I have icebergs to melt."

° ° °

George III had come out of the House of Lords after opening the session of Parliament. He met Lord Eldon and asked, "Lord Chancellor, did I deliver the speech well?"

"Very well indeed, sir," was the enthusiastic answer.

"I am glad of that," replied the king, "for there was nothing in it."

° ° °

At post-dinner speakers
I'm constantly balking
I'm through with my listening
Before they're through talking.

—D.E. Twiggs, Farm JNL

° ° °

Alfred E. Smith was being heckled at a large political gathering. "Go ahead Al—tell 'em all you know! It won't take long!" said the heckler.

Smith silenced him with: "I'll tell them all we both know. It won't take any longer."

—Saturday Evening Post

° ° °

In some respects a speech is like a love affair: any fool can start one, but to end it requires considerable skill.

—Britain's Lord Mancroft

° ° °

In my neighborhood, it is the gabbiest people who call themselves the silent majority.

° ° °

There would be not so many open mouths if there were not so many open ears.

° ° °

—Bishop Hall

° ° °

Eggheads unite—you have nothing to lose but your yolks.

—Adlai Stevenson

° ° °

He's a wonderful talker who has the art of telling you nothing in a great harangue.

— Jean Moliere

° ° °

Dentopedalogy is the science of opening your mouth and putting your foot in it. I've been practicing it for years.

—Philip, Duke of Edinburg

° ° °

Josh Billings once remarked that when some speakers strike oil they forget to stop boring. After an hour and a half of preaching, a clergyman who was given to both long and fanciful flights of oratory, was just getting warmed up to his theme of immortality.

"I looked up to the mountains," he shouted, "and I said, 'Mighty as you are, you will be destroyed; but my soul will not.' I gazed at the boundless ocean and cried, 'Vast as you are, you will some day dry up, but not I.' "

And then he wondered why his hearers laughed.

° ° °

With eggheads who try to be funny, the yolk usually breaks.

—Political opponent of Stevenson

° ° °

The habit of common and continuous speech is a symptom of mental deficiency.

—Bagehot

° ° °

Winston Churchill once gave this advice to speakers: "Don't be nervous. Do just as I do. Whenever I get up to speak I always make a point of taking a good look around the audience. I say to myself, 'What a lot of silly fools.' And then I always feel better."

o o o

He has a rage for saying something when there's nothing to be said.

—Samuel Johnson, referring to Warburton

o o o

He never speaks but his mouth opens.

—John Ray

o o o

I never give them hell. I just tell the truth, and they think it is hell.

—Harry S. Truman

o o o

See no evil, speak no evil, hear no evil, and half the women's clubs in the country will fold up within six weeks.

o o o

Half the trouble with the world today is due to the fact that far too many people are talking too much.

—Dr. Geoffrey Fisher, Archbishop of Canterbury

o o o

Conversation is the hare-brained chatter of irresponsible frivolity.

—Benjamin Disraeli

o o o

General Alexander Smyth, a tedious speaker in Congress, observed, "You, sir, speak for the present generation; but I speak for posterity."

"Yes," said Mr. Clay, "and you seem resolved to speak until the arrival of your audience."

—Henry Clay

o o o

The functions of the chairman are the same as the piece of parsley that is placed on top of a fish.

o o o

His argument is sound—only sound.

o o o

When Gladstone had finished a long speech in which he attacked the policies of Disraeli, the latter rose and said, "The man needs no reply. He is inebriated by the exuberance of his own verbosity."

o o o

THE POLITICAL ARENA
Introduction

The political arena has been termed the Mad World of Nimble Nonsense. A Russian proverb states: "Politics is a rotten egg; if broken open, it stinks."

No doubt there is an orgy of corruption in political life. This unfortunate truth becomes evident when we see that the "ins" want to stay in, and the "outs" want to get in. No wonder, when a politician is out to get votes, he is convertible.

Jay Gould, once the boss of the Erie Railroad, remarked, "In a Republican district I was a Republican. In a Democratic district, I was a Democrat. And in a doubtful district I was doubtful. But I was always for Erie."

It doesn't matter who you read, or what you read—all through the ages disenchanted observations have been made by a variety of writers and speakers, from Confucius to Marx (Groucho). Some of these remarks were humorous, others were classics of irony; still others were just dyspeptic. What greater affront can be used on politicians than to use the words of Robert Louis Stevenson: "Politics is perhaps the only profession for which no preparation is thought necessary."

Mark Twain, more than once indicated in his own humorous, sarcastic way what he thought about politicians and government leaders. He compared legislators to idiots and apes. He looked at politicians as one sees apes and chimpanzees in a zoo. "When Congress is in session," he said, "I have plenty of humor for my column." He went on to devastate them with "Reader, suppose you were an idiot; and suppose you were a member of Congress; but I repeat myself."

Politicians, sooner or later, fall into disrepute. Whether he makes wise decisions or unpopular ones, he is taken over the coals. He is the voter's scapegoat, the gagster's meat, and the comedian's vehicle through which laughs can be gotten. Like the prostitute, he is universally condemned, but often called upon.

Yet, politicians have earned a place for themselves in history. Some have made enviable reputations. How wise was Ben Franklin when he wrote: "The first mistake in public business is the getting into it." He never took his own advice in this matter. Any person entering politics must bear in mind Oliver's summation of politicians. He wrote: "Politicians are like pendants in Montaigne's essays; no one has a good word for them."

It is difficult to believe that the United States Senate is sometimes referred to as "The Zoo," and the House of Representatives is sometimes called, "The Monkey House." It is, however, understandable when you think of some of those who have been members of the illustrious houses.

Mark Twain summed it up in the words: "It could probably be shown by facts and figures that there is no distinctively native criminal class except Congress."

In the pages that follow you will find a variety of invectives, affronts, insults, bristles, poison darts, and sharp verbal arrows. Read them for what they're worth. Some will give inspiration; others, stimulation; and still others, valued insights. To all I say, as they call out at some auctions, "You pays your money and you takes the pick."

So laugh along!

THE POLITICAL ARENA

o o o

Just for a handful of silver he left us,
Just for a ribbon to stick in his coat.

—Browning, The Lost Leader

o o o

Politicans treat Americans as jackasses because they think we are, and we don't tell them any different.

—Mark VanDoren

o o o

I never said all Democrats were saloonkeepers; what I said was all saloonkeepers were Democrats.

—Horace Greeley

o o o

If the Republicans stop telling lies about us, we will stop telling the truth about them.

—Adlai Stevenson

o o o

It is a tragedy that the Old Guard has succeeded in doing what Hitler's best general never could do: They captured Eisenhower.

—Adlai Stevenson Time,11/3/52

o o o

As to their platform, well, nobody can stand on a bushel of eels.

—Adlai Stevenson comment on Republican platform

o o o

Politics is the diversion of trivial men who, when they succeed at it, become important in the eyes of more trivial men.

—George Jena Nathan

o o o

Politicians are the same all over. They promise to build a bridge even where there is no river.

—Nikita Khrushchev, N.Y. Herald Tribune, Aug. 22, 1963

o o o

A politician is a man who approaches every subject with an open mouth.

—Tom Connolly

o o o

Politicians are like the bones of a horse's fore-shoulder—not a straight one in it.

—Wendell Philips

o o o

He is one of those political candidates who refuses to answer any question on the ground that it will eliminate him.

o o o

He's a politician who can shake your hand in the fall, and then shake your faith in the spring.

o o o

The only thing he can raise in this land is taxes.

o o o

I am not a politician, and my other habits are good.

—Artemus Ward

o o o

A whale's tongue is found to contain 8% of the oil in his system. In politicians, the proportion is even higher.

o o o

I'm not a politician. I've only got one face.

—Brendan Behan

o o o

One of them is a politician, the other is an honest individual.

—Brendan Behan

o o o

Timid and interested politicians think much more about the security of their sets than about the security of their country.

—T. B. Macaulay, House of Commons

o o o

In politics there is no honor.

—Benjamin Disraeli

o o o

Damn your principles! Stick to your party.

° ° °

—Disraeli to Bulwer-Lytton

° ° °

Those who are in Albany escaped Sing Sing, and those who are in Sing Sing were on their way to Albany.

—Elbert Hubbard, Book of Epigrams

° ° °

They are playing politics at the expense of human misery.

° ° °

Politics is perhaps the only profession for which no preparation is thought necessary.

—Robert L. Stevenson

° ° °

Politics is the art of governing mankind by deceiving them.

—Isaac Disraeli, Curiosities of Literature

° ° °

Politician: A guy who contrasts his wings and halo against his opponent's horn and tail.

° ° °

Politics is the art of looking for trouble, finding it everywhere, diagnosing it wrongly, and applying unsuitable remedies.

—Sir Ernest Benn

° ° °

Politics: A profession holding out the greatest amount of power for the least amount of training or responsibility.

° ° °

Politics has three sides to it: the right side, the wrong side, and the way it really happened.

° ° °

His political consistency was only the product of a dull mind.

° ° °

The President and the press.
Two on a seesaw.

—Kermit Lansner

° ° °

"Senator, a lot of your constituents can't understand from your speech last night just how you stand on the question."

"Fine! It took me seven hours to write it that way."

° ° °

Maybe politicians don't duel the way they seem to, but they sure can fence.

° ° °

If a politician had to stand on the planks of his platform it would be constructed better.

° ° °

Our political leadership today consists of a few great, a few near great, many who think they are great, and those who just grate.

—William G. Mather

° ° °

Politics is developing more comedians than radio ever did.

—Jimmy Durante

° ° °

When a politician promises you "something for nothing," you can be pretty sure that he will get a lot for "something" and that you will get a lot of "nothing."

° ° °

When a politician starts shedding tears, it's certain that somebody's water taxes go up.

—Ronald Colman

° ° °

Drew Pearson is the scorpion-on-the Potomac!

° ° °

Pearson is an infamous liar, a revolting liar,a pusillanimous liar, a lying ass, a natural born liar, a liar by profession, a liar of living, a liar in the daytime, a liar in the nighttime, a dishonest, ignorant, corrupt and groveling crook.

—Senator Kenneth McKellar

° ° °

Congress was run by a group of old men from small towns... a council of elders whose only claim to power is their ability to outlive their colleagues.

—Drew Pearson

° ° °

Joseph R. McCarthy was a demagogic genie out of a bottle.

—Drew Pearson

° ° °

Everyone makes mistakes... but this S.O.B. makes a racket, a business, a mint of money writing fiction in the guise of news reporting.

—Walter Winchell about Drew Pearson

° ° °

He is a miscalled newscaster specializing in falsehoods.

—Westbrook Pegler about Drew Pearson

° ° °

He will go down in history as Pearson-the-sponge, because he gathers slime, mud and slander from all parts of the earth and lets the mud ooze out through his radio broadcasts and through his daily contributions to a few newspapers which have not found him out yet.

—Senator Theodor Bilbo of Mississippi

• • •

No S.O.B. like Pearson is going to prevail on me to discharge anyone by some smart-aleck statement over the air.

—Harry Truman, about Pearson who wanted Gen. Harry H. Vaughan to be fired

• • •

Interrupting a bumbling colleague: "If the distinguished Senator will allow me, I will try to extricate him from his thoughts."

—Senator Eugene Millikin

• • •

If I were in Parliament I would write on my forehead, "To Let." Add, "Unfurnished," was the rejoinder.

• • •

This devil of a man (Poincare) is the opposite of Briand: The latter knows nothing, and understands everything; the other knows everything and understands nothing.

—George Clemenceau

• • •

He looks as if he had been weaned on a pickle.

—Alice Roosevelt Longworth, about Calvin Coolidge

• • •

He is humorless to the point of being inhuman. He is devious. He is vacillating. He is profane. He is willing to be led. He displays dismaying gaps in knowledge. He is suspicious of his staff. His loyalty is minimal.

—Chicago Tribune, about Nixon

• • •

The Watergate transcripts revealed deplorable, disgusting, shabby, immoral performances by everyone involved, not excluding the President.

—Hugh Scott, Senate Minority Leader

• • •

He is a great unrecognized incapacity.

—Carl Otto, Prince von Bismark about Napoleon

• • •

He is a sheep in sheep's clothing.

—Winston Churchill, on Clemont Atlee

° ° °

Baldwin occasionally stumbles over the truth, but he always hastily picks himself up and hurries on as if nothing had happened.

—Winston Churchill about Sir Stafford Cripps

° ° °

Walking in the street one day, Lord Chesterfield was pushed off the pavement by an enemy who said, "I never give the wall to a scoundrel."

Replied Lord Chesterfield, "Sir, I always do."

° ° °

America is a society of simple answers to complex questions —all of which are wrong.

° ° °

Being in government requires the technique of saying what you don't mean and making it mean who you don't say.

° ° °

Some of these people setting out to clean up the world ought to start off by taking a bath.

—Will Durant

° ° °

There, but for the grace of God, goes God.

—Winston Churchil about Sir Stafford Cripps

° ° °

The Earl of Lauderdale laughed boisterously at a joke of Richard Brinsley Sheridan and said he'd have to remember it to repeat it. Replied Sheridan, "Ray don't, my dear Lauderdale: a joke in your mouth is no laughing matter."

° ° °

There is only one way to look at a politician and that's down.

—Mark Twain

° ° °

In his 30 years in Washington, Humphrey has done the work of two men—Laurel and Hardy.

—About Senator Hubert Humphrey

° ° °

Ronald Reagan started out as an underweight, inexperienced dishwasher in Amlico, Illinois. Unfortunately, he never lived up to his early promise.

—At a "Roaster " gathering

° ° °

Pearson is the most colossal liar in the world.

—Hamilton Fish

° ° °

A man can build a staunch reputation for honesty by admitting he was in error, especially when he gets caught at it.

—Robert Ruark about Ted Kennedy

o o o

Pearson is a miscalled newscaster specializing in falsehoods and smearing people with personal and political motivation.

—Westbrook Pegler

o o o

The only difference between a rut and a grave is their dimensions.

—Ellen Glasgow about a conservative

o o o

If politicians were investigated, most of them would be running for the border.

o o o

The reason politicians always stand on their record is to keep the public from examining it.

o o o

Now and then an innocent man is sent to the legislature.

—Frank McKinney

o o o

Political promises go in one year and out the other.

o o o

Corruption is no stranger to Washington; its a famous resident.

—Walter Goodman

o o o

A political war is one in which everyone shoots from the lip.

—Raymond Moley

o o o

Politics is the gentle art of getting votes from poor and campaign funds from the rich, by promises to protect each from the other.

—Oscar Ameringer 1870-1943

o o o

A Parliament is nothing less than•a big meeting of more or less idle people.

o o o

I think the man who is out of public life is a most fortunate person, for the reason that it is an era of intellectual dishonesty and hypocrisy.

—James M. Cox

o o o

The famous politician was trying to save both his faces.

—John Gunther

° ° °

To be a chemist you must study chemistry; to be a lawyer or a physician you must study law or medicine; but to be a politician you need only to study your own interests.

—Max O'Rell

° ° °

The great difficulty with politics is that there are no established principles.

—Napoleon Bonaparte

° ° °

Party spirit enlists a man's virtues in the cause of his vices.

—Richard Whately

° ° °

Two kinds of men generally best succeed in political life: men of no principle, but of great talent; and men of no talent, but of one principle—that of obedience to their superiors.

—Wendell Phillips

° ° °

A scurvy lot they are (in the United States Senate) are they not, with their smirking and cringing and voluble palaver about God and patriotism and their eager offerings of endowments for hospitals and colleges whenever the American people so much as looks hard in their direction!

—David Graham Phillips *The Treason of the Senate*

° ° °

Politics is a tug of war between people who want to get in and people who don't want to get out.

° ° °

Political platforms are for one party to stand on, and the other to jump on.

—Arnold H. Glasow

° ° °

Power, like a desloating pestilence,
Pollutes whate'er it touches.

—Percy B. Shelley

° ° °

Politicans promise the people a car in every garage and after election build parking meters.

° ° °

It is important for a politician to have a long nose since he can't see beyond it.

° ° °

Though I have been in politics for well over forty years, I loathe the professional politician.

—Mayor F. La Guardia 1882-1947

o o o

One of the principle qualifications for a political job is that the applicant know nothing about what he is expected to do.

o o o

You cannot adopt politics as a profession and remain honest.

—Louis McHenry Howe

o o o

Under the Empress' shirt there is only the naked skin.

o o o

Laws rule people and gold rules laws.

o o o

Expect nothing from the politician who promises a great deal.

o o o

He who serves the public hath but a scurvy master. Marble polished is neither less hard nor less cold; so with courtiers.

o o o

Neither politics nor revolution shows any mercy to the lives and fortunes of men.

—Svetlana Alliluyeve Stalin in *Twenty Letters to a Friend*

o o o

Nowhere are prejudices more mistaken for truth, passion for reason, and invective for documentation than in politics.

—John Mason Brown in *Through These Men*

o o o

Politics is the means by which the will of the few becomes the will of the many.

—Howard Koch and John Huston in *In Time to Come*

o o o

The American people, true enough, are sheep. Worse, they are donkeys. Yet worse, to borrow from their own dialect, they are goats. They are thus constantly bamboozled and exploited by small minorities of their own number.

—H. L. Mencken *Notes on Democracy*

o o o

Practical politics consists in ignoring facts.

—Henry Adams

o o o

Politics is like roller skating. You go partly where you want to go, and partly where the damned things take you.

—Henry Ashurst

o o o

The punishment which the wise suffer, who refuse to take part in the government, is to live under the government of worse men.

—Ralph Waldo Emerson

° ° °

Politics is the art of governing mankind by deceiving them.

—Isaac Disraeli *Curiosities of Literature*

° ° °

Politicians love a wordy cause.

° ° °

A politician should have three hats. One for throwing in the ring, one for talking through, and one for pulling rabbits out of, if elected.

—Carl Sandburg

° ° °

Politics is dirty, Congress is undemocratic; our class leadership is inept.

—David T. Bazelon

° ° °

An honest election, under democracy, is an act of innocence which does not take place more than once in the history of a given nation.

—Jose Maria Gil Robles

° ° °

There is no more independence in politics than there is in jail.

—Will Rogers

° ° °

A politician weakly and amiably in the right, is no match for a politician tenaciously and pugnaciously in the wrong.

—Edwin Percey Whipple

° ° °

Politicians. Little Tin Gods on Wheels.

—Rudyard Kipling

° ° °

A dead politician is the noblest work of God.

° ° °

The politician is an acrobat. He keeps his balance by saying the opposite of what he does.

—Maurice Barres

° ° °

Be a politician; no training necessary.

—Will Rogers

° ° °

Government under democracy is thus government by orgy, almost by orgasm.

—H.L. Mencken

° ° °

In politics the choice is constantly between two evils.

—John Morley

° ° °

If you do not know how to lie, cheat and steal, turn your attention to politics and learn.

—Josh Billings

° ° °

Once a man holds public office he is absolutely no good for honest work.

Ibid

° ° °

Political elections . . . are a good deal like marriages, there's no accounting for anyone's taste.

° ° °

A diplomatic language has a hundred ways of saying nothing but no way of saying something.

Ibid

° ° °

Diplomats are nothing but high class lawyers. Some ain't even high class.

Ibid

° ° °

Alexander Hamilton originated the "put and take" system into our national treasury. The taxpayers put it in and the politicians take it out.

Ibid

° ° °

Washington was elected the first President because he was about the only one who had enough money to give a decent inauguration party.

Ibid

° ° °

Politics, as the word is commonly understood, are nothing but corruptions.

—Jonathan Swift in *Thoughts on Various Subjects*

° ° °

. . . that insidious and crafty animal, vulgarly called a statesman or politician, whose councils are directed by the momentary fluctuations of affairs.

—Adam Smith

o o o

Whenever a man has cast a longing eye on offices, a rottenness begins in his conduct.

—Thomas Jefferson

o o o

The northern Democrats squabble with the Southern Democrats, and Modern Republicans wrangle with the Old Guard. This is known as a 2-party system or a 3-ring circus.

o o o

Only the Democratic party would hold a dinner at which the speakers so nearly outnumber the audience.

—Senator Hubert Humphrey

o o o

If you lie with dogs, you rise with fleas.

o o o

He didn't carve his career, he chiseled it.

—Walter Winchell

o o o

Jack Kennedy' father: "Jack, what do you want as a career?"
Jack Kennedy: "I want to be president."
Jack Kennedy's father: "I know about that—but I mean when you grow up."

—Republican National Committee Magazine

o o o

An anonymous congressman, commenting on the story that Rep. Adam Clayton Powell (D.-NY.) gave his secretary a $9,000 raise after he married her: "Adam must have promised to love, honor and over-pay."

o o o

What this state (Illinois) needs is a strong dose of electoral DDT.

—Adlai Stevenson

o o o

A mugwump is a person educated beyond his intellect.

—Horace Porter, Blaine Campaign

o o o

The mistake a lot of politicians make is in forgetting they've been appointed and thinking they've been anointed.

—Ms. Claude Pepper

o o o

As a politician he is an acrobat; he stands on the fence while keeping one ear to the ground.

o o o

Politics makes strange bedfellows, but they soon get accustomed to the same bunk.

o o o

I cussed out old McCarthy every chance I got. He was nothing but a damn coward, and he was afraid of me. The only thing he ever did that I approved of was when he knocked down Drew Pearson.

—Harry S. Truman

o o o

The President of the United States, a man nobody writes off as a political scientist is gambling that McCarthy is an overrated punk.

—Murry Kempton about Harry S. Truman

o o o

If I don't like creeping socialism, there's something else I dislike just as much—and that's galloping reaction.

—Adlai Stevenson

o o o

Meetings consisting of some half a dozen scurvy pot-house politicians.

—Washington Irving

o o o

One of the evils of democracy is that you have to endure the man you elected whether you like him or not.

—Will Rogers

o o o

Politicians get into the public eye by prying into the public chest.

o o o

Politicians have what it takes to take what you've got.

o o o

Politicans are people who have careers of a promising nature.

o o o

A politician is an arse upon which every one has sat except a man.

—e. e. cummings

o o o

A good politician is quite as unthinkable as an honest burglar.

—H. L. Mencken

o o o

We must indeed all hang together, or most assuredly we shall all hang separately.

—Benjamin Franklin

o o o

To be able to endure odium is the first art to be learned by those who aspire to power.

—Seneca

° ° °

A politician . . . one that would circumvent God.

—William Shakespeare

° ° °

Democracy substitutes the election by the incompetent many for appointment by the corrupt few.

—George Bernard Shaw

° ° °

Fate often makes up for the eminence of the office by the inferiority of the officeholder.

—Baaltasar Gracian

° ° °

A national campaign is better than the best circus ever heard of, with a mass baptism and a couple of hangings thrown in. It is better, even than war.

° ° °

That politician tops his part,
Who readily can lie with art;
That man's proficient in his trade;
His pow'r is strong, his fortune's made.

—John Gay

° ° °

In politics nothing is contemptible.

—Benjamin Disraeli

° ° °

All political parties die at last of swallowing their own lies.

—John Arbuthnot

° ° °

It is not so much that Stevenson is funny as that other politicians are dull.

—Christian Science Monitor

° ° °

An honest politician is one who when he is bought stays bought.

° ° °

I am considerably concerned when I see the extent to which we are developing a one-party press in a two-party country.

—Adlai Stevenson

° ° °

The Republican party is half McCarthy and half-Free.

—Adlai Stevenson

° ° °

A Conservative is a man who is too cowardly to fight and too fat to run.

—Elbert Hubbard

° ° °

Mr. Truman is a part-time President of the White House and he has "a lamentable penchant for meddling with an historic structure which the nation prefers as it is."

—*New York Herald Tribune*

° ° °

There were some very good men in the Senate; most of them were, but there were some who were not so good, who were lazy, who never did any work but who got the headlines every time they made a speech, and some of them got sent back to the Senate time after time.

—Harry S. Truman

° ° °

Some people come to Washington and grow with their jobs, but a lot of others come, and all they do is swell up.

—Woodrow Wilson

° ° °

. . . It makes no difference if the billionaire rode to wealth on the sweat of little children and the blood of underpaid labor . . . No one ever considers the Carnegie libraries steeped in the blood of the Homestead steel workers, but they are. We do not remember that the Rockefeller Foundation is founded on the dead miners of the Colorado Fuel Company and a dozen other performances. We worship Mamon . . .

—Harry S. Truman

° ° °

I discovered after some time that Chaing Kai-shek and the Madame and their families, the Soong family and the Kungs, were all thieves, every last one of them, the Madame and him included. And they stole seven hundred and fifty million dollars out of the thirty-five billion we sent to Chiang. They stole it, and it's invested in real estate down in Sao Paulo and some right here in New York.

—Harry S. Truman about Chiang Kai-shek

° ° °

What he said he wasn't going to do was exactly what I knew he was going to do. I don't know, in Henry's case, if you'd say he was a liar as much as that; he didn't know the difference between the truth and a lie.

—Ibid

° ° °

I fired him because he wouldn't respect the authority of the President. That's the answer to that. I didn't fire him because he was a dumb son-of-a-bitch, although he was, but that's not against the law for generals. If it was, half to three-quarters of them would be in jail.

—Harry S. Truman about General MacArthur

° ° °

I have never been more disappointed in a public official. He was a muddled, totally irrational man, almost incapable of uttering a coherent sentence. He was also the bitterest man I have ever encountered.

—Harry S. Truman about Henry Wallace

° ° °

The trouble with Ickes was . . . well, he was no better than a common cold. I don't like saying that about a man, but it's true, and he wanted to be President the worst way.

—Harry S. Truman, about Harold Ickes

° ° °

When Douglas accused Abraham Lincoln of being two-faced, Lincoln replied, "Do you think if I had two faces I'd be wearing this one?"

° ° °

He is a lame duck and is in the process of becoming a cooked goose.

° ° °

A politician who had changed his views rather radicallly was congratulated by a colleague who said, "I'm glad you've seen the light!"

"I didn't see the light," came back the reply, "I felt the heat!"

° ° °

"Hold my horse for a minute, will you?"

"Sir, I'll have you know that I am a member of Congress!"

"Oh, that's all right! I'll trust you."

° ° °

Trying to solve the country's problems with Congressional oratory is like trying to untangle a traffic jam by honking the horn.

° ° °

There's one thing you can say about the Republicans running this government; they're running it like nobody's business.

° ° °

"Status quo," said the candidate for Mayor, "is just another name for the mess we're in."

° ° °

"If you don't want to go to Heaven, and you don't want to go to Hell," thundered the evangelist, "where do you want to go?"

"To Congress," replied the candidate for office.

° ° °

To build an "ethical stonewall" around President Nixon at this point would require a Merlin of a stonemason. Father John McLaughlin is merely an apprentice bricklayer with a forked tongue for a trowel and hot air for mortar.

—*Newsweek*

° ° °

Congress is now confronted with the unsolved problem of how to get the people to pay taxes they can't afford for services they don't really need.

° ° °

My opponent will have you believe that he is thinking when all he is doing is rearranging his prejudices.

° ° °

William Howard Taft was facing an unfriendly audience. He finally appealed to the presiding officer, saying: "I have been talking for a quarter of an hour, but there is so much noise that I can hardly hear myself talk."

"That's all right," shouted someone from the rear; "you're not missing anything."

° ° °

When Talleyrand was told that the Abbey Sieys was a very profound man, he replied:

"Profound! Yes, he is a perfect cavity!"

° ° °

And like the scurvy politician, seem
To see the things thou dost not.

—Shakespeare in *King Lear*

° ° °

A horse, a cow, and a donkey were debating about which had made the greatest contribution to the war.

The horse claimed first honors, because he made it possible for the men to ride off to war and haul their cannon into position.

The cow said that were it not that she had stayed home, the civilian population would have starved within three months, and the war brought to an end.

But the donkey said very boastfully, "None of you contributed as much as I, for had I not been in the diplomacy at the head of the governments, there would never have been a war!"

° ° °

At least 90% of efforts to be funny flop. Of course, Washington, D.C. has a better percentage.

o o o

Since man is the only animal that can be skinned more than once, we have politicians instead of statesmen.

o o o

A hat is something the average man covers his head with, the beggar passes around, the statesman throws into the ring, and the politician talks through.

o o o

There was a time when it cost more to feed the bugs and insects in this country than it did to run the government, but in the last ten years the government has caught up.

o o o

He is a man of splendid abilities, but utterly corrupt. Like a rotten mackerel by moonlight, he shines and stinks.

—John Randolph about Edward Livingston

o o o

He is an infernal scoundrel but that is his only fault.

—J. M. Barrie about the German Kaiser

o o o

At one time the House of Commons had sat in a long and ineffectual session. Mr. Papham, speaker of the House of Commons, was summoned by the Queen and asked, "Now Mr. Speaker, what has passed in the Commons' House?"

He replied, "If it please Your Majesty—seven weeks."

o o o

A doctor, an engineer and a politician were arguing which profession was the oldest.

Doctor: "Mine is. God's operation making Eve out of Adam's rib."

Engineer: "Mine is. Creation was made out of chaos."

Politician: "But who created the chaos?"

o o o

You cannot eradicate disease from the human body unless you eradicate it from the body politic.

—Louis D. Brandeis

o o o

Politics is the career of plundering and blundering.

—Disraeli letter to Lord Grey de Wilton

o o o

Lord Chatham commented about an approaching debate. "If I canot speak standing I will speak sitting, and If I cannot speak sitting, I will speak lying."

"Which he will do in whatever position he speaks," commented Lord North.

o o o

When a certain politician was spoken of as being capable of assassinating anyone, Talleyrand commented: "Assassinating, no! Poisoning, yes!"

o o o

Politicians are getting so high priced they have to be rented instead of bought.

o o o

Winston Churchill was accused by a Laborite of "lying" in the House of Commons. Churchill demanded that the Laborite repeat his exact words and was mollified when, for the word "lie," he substituted the Victorian phrase, "terminological inexactitude."

o o o

A candidate for office once asked a tradesman for his vote. The tradesman answered, "I admire your abilities, but damn your principles." To which the candidate replied, "My friend, I applaud your sincerity, but damn your manners."

o o o

Adlai Stevenson was a man who could never make up his mind whether he had to go to the bathroom or not.

—Harry S. Truman

o o o

Henry Wallace was a fellow who wanted to be a great man but didn't know how to go about it.

—Harry S. Truman

o o o

Mr. Luce, a man like you must have trouble sleeping at night. Because your job is to inform people, but what you do is misinform them.

—Harry S. Truman about Henry Luce

o o o

If Patrick Henry thought taxation without representation was bad, he ought to see it with representation.

o o o

Politics: the art of looking for trouble, finding it everywhere, diagnosing it incorrectly, and applying the wrong remedies.

—Groucho Marx

o o o

These are exciting days in Washington. Some are getting posts while others are getting the gate.

o o o

My opponent wraps himself up in the flimsy garment of his own righteousness and then complains of the cold.

° ° °

If you owe 275 dollars you're a piker; if you owe 275 thousand dollars you're a business man; if you owe 275 million dollars you're a tycoon and if you owe 275 billion you're the government.

° ° °

Governor Giles of Virginia once wrote to Patrick Henry demanding satisfaction: Sir, I understand that you have called me a "bob-tail" politician. I wish to know if it be true; and if true, your meaning.

—William B. Giles

° ° °

To which Mr. Henry replied:

Sir, I do not recollect having called you a bob-tail politician at any time but think it probable I have. Not recollecting the time or occasion I can't say what I mean, but if you will tell me what you think I meant, I will say whether you are correct. Very respectfully,

—Patrick Henry

° ° °

When a politician repairs his fence, he sometimes finds a hedge more useful.

° ° °

Imagination is what makes some politicians think they're statesmen.

° ° °

Practical politics consists of ignoring the facts.

—Henry Adams

° ° °

Tiresome politicians, during a debate: "I will bet my head that you are wrong."

Second politician: "I accept it. The smallest trifle has its value among friends."

° ° °

Old politicians never die; they just run once too often.

° ° °

One Democratic automobile, the Hubert, designed as the plain people's car, known as the Folks Wagon, has been withdrawn from the race, which is a pity, for it had acceleration. From a standing start, it could roar up to 300 words a minute in five seconds.

—Republic Senator Kenneth Keating

° ° °

He is a crafty politican asking for the floor and taking the whole house.

° ° °

Politics is the only profession in which mediocrities can gain the world's attention through slander.

° ° °

I have spent much of my life fighting the Germans and fighting the politicians. It is much easier to fight the Germans.

—Field Marshal Lord Montgomery

° ° °

The Democratic Party is not one but two political parties with the same name. They unite only once every two years to wage political campaigns.

—Dwight D. Eisenhower

° ° °

He is the type of political candidate who started by trying to move mountains but ended up by merely throwing dirt.

° ° °

I've got no degrees except that I didn't earn.

—Harry S. Truman, a lecturer at Columbia Univ.

° ° °

Life is not a static thing. The only people who do not change their minds are incompetents in asylums, who can't, and those in cemeteries.

—Sen. Everett Dirksen, Senate Minority Leader

° ° °

The other side can have a monopoly on all the dirt in this campaign.

—Grover Cleveland during campaign of 1884

° ° °

Nixon is a household name; so is garbage.

° ° °

John Lindsay? After his record in New York, even if he runs unopposed, he'll lose.

° ° °

A funny thing happened to Vice President Agnew last week —he opened his mouth and a foot fell out.

° ° °

He is the kind of politician who could cut down a redwood tree, then mount the stump and make a speech for conservation.

—Adlai Stevenson about Nixon

° ° °

I'm proud that I am a politician. It takes politicians to run a government. A statesman is a politician who has been dead for 10 or 15 years.

—Harry S. Truman

° ° °

The senator was campaigning for reelection in a rural section of the country. His long-winded address had been going on and on, with brief stops for gulps of water. During one of these brief pauses, an old farmer turned on his engine and said, "First time I ever saw a windmill run by water."

° ° °

In some African countries a man can't hold an office until he has shot a rhinoceros. Over here, voters consider a man qualified if he can shoot the bull.

° ° °

The world is weary of statesmen whom democracy has degraded into politicians.

—Disraeli

° ° °

A conservative is a man with two perfectly good legs who, however, has never learned to walk.

—Franklin D. Roosevelt

° ° °

Gov.Romney says he writes his own speeches. Well, it's nice of him not to blame anyone else.

—Quote

° ° °

The Vice-Presidency isn't worth a pitcher of warm spit.

—Vice-President Nance Garner to V.P. Lyndon Johnson

° ° °

Being Governor of Michigan is like being the quarterback of a team chosen by your opponents.

—George Romney

° ° °

I sincerely fear for my country if Jack Kennedy should be elected president. The fellow has absolutely no principles. Money and gall are all the Kennedys have.

—Barry Goldwater as told to Westbrook Pegler

° ° °

Ambassador Kennedy is known to American correspondents as "Nitery Joe."

—Victor Bienstock

° ° °

... Like Huey Long (senator from Louisiana) who was later assassinated. He was a liar, and he was nothing but a damn demagogue. It didn't surprise me when they shot him. These demagogues, the ones that live by demagoguery. They all end up the same way.

—Harry S. Truman

° ° °

If the Congress isn't a bit more cautious, they will carry this welfare idea too far. Living conditions will improve so much that we're going to run out of humble beginnings for our great men!

° ° °

A platform is getting to be something a candidate stands on before election, and falls down on afterward.

° ° °

When friends told John Quincy Adams that a young congressman was ridiculing him on account of his age, near 80 at that time, the venerable old politician remarked slyly, "Tell that young man that an ass is older at thirty than a man is at eighty."

° ° °

Sen. Karl Mundt suggested that the then Interior Secretary Stewart L. Udall and other government officials wear mint-flavored shoes since they are continually finding their feet in their mouths.

° ° °

Being Vice-President is like adding maternity benefits to Social Security—you're there, but nobody needs you.

—Spiro T. Agnew

° ° °

I'm going to introduce a resolution to have the Postmaster General stop reading dirty books and deliver the mail.

—Senator Gale McGee

° ° °

William Saxbe has developed an obnoxious habit of letting his tongue flap without using his brain.

—*Daily News* Editorial

° ° °

The other night I dreamed that I was addressing the House of Lords. Then I woke up and by God I was.

—Duke of Devonshire

° ° °

Behind the closed door of his office, he seems both more human and far less commanding—a muddled thinker, a rambling talker, a waffling executive, a president who instead of presiding at these critical discussions, defers continuously to his subordinates.

—*Newsweek* May 13, 1974 Nixon Tapes

o o o

He's a big clown.

—Nixon about F.B.I. Director L. Patrick Gray

o o o

It is difficult to feel compassion for an attorney who is so morally obtuse, that he consciously cheats for his own pecuniary gain, that Government he has sworn to serve.

—*Newsweek* May 13, 1974

o o o

Forrestal was hounded to his death by Pearson with vicious lies until his reason broke and he jumped out of a high window.

—Westbrook Pegler

o o o

The Salvation Army bra (uplifts the fallen), the Communist bra (supports the masses) and the Drew Pearson bra (makes mountains out of molehills).

o o o

What would happen if Sherman Adams died and Eisenhower became President?

—Drew Pearson about Eisenhower's advisor, Adams

o o o

Nixon was working for his ambition until he became President. Now he is working for the history books. It may be premature to dismiss him as just another Herbert Hoover.

—Drew Pearson

o o o

Forrestal is a bureaucratic voice for American oil companies with enormous stakes in the Mideast.

—Drew Pearson

o o o

My opponent boasts that he is a hard-boiled egg. Well, folks, I never saw a hard-boiled egg that didn't have a yellow heart.

—Former Gov. Jack Walton, Oklahoma

o o o

When he gets started, his tongue is like a race horse; it runs faster the less weight it carries.

—Sen. Carter Glass

o o o

Winston Churchill once blandly remarked of a parliamentary opponent that he had missed a very fine opportunity for keeping quiet.

o o o

DeGaulle's historical record may be that, as a writer, he wrote too little, as a soldier he fought too little, and as a statesman, he came too late.

—Brian Crozier, Author

o o o

I don't want to be President again because there's no chance for advancement.

—Calvin Coolidge

o o o

Hoover never was a Great Humanitarian, a Great Administrator, a Great Engineer or a great anything.

—Robert S. Allen

o o o

I was offered the ambassadorship of Liberia once, when the post was earmarked for a Negro. I told them I wouldn't take a Jim Crow job.

—Ralph Bunche

o o o

When the history of this Republic shall be written, Woodrow Wilson's titanic figure will tower above the puny Pygmies who now bark at his memory as Pike's Peak towers above the fog of an Arkansas swamp.

—Tom Connally, Rep. 1916-28, Sen. 1928-52.

o o o

There is one columnist in Washington who wouldn't have room on his breast if he got a ribbon for every time he's called a liar. In Missouri we have a four-letter word for those who knowingly make false statements.

—President Truman about Drew Pearson

o o o

If anything happens to Nixon the secret service men have orders to shoot Agnew.

—Told about Agnew when he was Vice President

o o o

He makes America sound like the Land of Promise—especially before Election Day.

o o o

If we could use the money that political candidates spend on their campaigns, all the ills they speak about could be cured.

o o o

The candidate for Mayor had a secret popularity poll taken. Now he wants to make sure it's kept that way.

o o o

He speaks his mind, but unfortunately that limits the conversation.

° ° °

Two state senators were talking about some upcoming bills. "What should I do about this prostitution bill?" the younger senator asked. "Pay it!" answered his colleague.

° ° °

When it was demanded of a newspaper to retract the statement it had printed *"Half of the city officials are crooks,"* they retracted with, *"Half of the city officials aren't crooks."*

° ° °

A critic of the State Department says it either ought to improve on its predictions or register as a non-prophet organization.

—*Quote* July 16, 1967

° ° °

Stevenson let it be known that he knew the real reason why Ike had decided to run for a second term. He (Ike) can't afford to retire to his Gettysburg farm as long as Ezra Benson is Sec. of Agriculture.

° ° °

I know Gov. Thomas E. Dewey and Mr. Dewey is a fine man. Yes, Dewey is a fine man. So is my Uncle Morris. My Uncle Morris shouldn't be president; neither should Dewey.

—George Jessel

° ° °

When the late Henry Wallace was U.S. Secretary of Agriculture, he was once heckled by a farmer. Wallace had just said, "This country should raise more wheat." "What about hay?" asked the heckler. "I'm speaking about food for mankind, but I'll get around to your case in a minute," Wallace replied.

° ° °

I am grateful for the overwhelming vote of confirmation in the Senate. We must now wait until the dirt settles. My difficulties, of course, go back some years back when Senator Wayne Morse was kicked in the head by a horse.

—Clare Booth Luce, statement made after Senate confirmed her nomination as Ambassador to Brazil.

° ° °

It is only governments that are stupid, not the masses of people.

—President Eisenhower

° ° °

I feel like the fellow in jail who is watching his scaffold being built.

—Pres. Eisenhower, commenting on the construction of the reviewing stands for Kennedy's inauguration.

° ° °

Khrushchev reminds me of the tiger hunter who has picked a place on the wall to hang the tiger's skin long before he has caught the tiger. This tiger has other ideas.

—Pres. Kennedy, *N.Y. Times* Dec. 24, 1961

° ° °

You don't set a fox to watching the chickens just because he has a lot of experience in the hen house.

—Harry Truman about Nixon

° ° °

I've never met him (Vice-President Ford) but I used to spend time in Ohio, and they turn out Jerry Fords by the bale.

—Alice Roosevelt Longworth

° ° °

There's no other country with as much air, and not knowing where it's going, as this country.

—Will Rogers

° ° °

We know that there are chiselers. At the bottom of every case of criticism and obstruction we have found some selfish interest, some private axe to grind.

—F.D. Roosevelt, Speech 1936

° ° °

Chancellor Gerhard's politics remind me of a lump of dough; they are just as soft and always in the shape produced by outside pressure.

—Dr. W. Stammberger,
West German Bundestag

° ° °

If you can't stand the heat, stay out of the kitchen.

—Harry Truman to his cabinet

° ° °

I keep my words soft, honeyed, and warm, because I never know when I may be called upon to eat them.

—Sen. Everett Dirksen

° ° °

Stevenson is a Harry Truman with table manners.

° ° °

I can either run the country or control Alice (his daughter) but not both.

—Theodore Roosevelt

° ° °

If the damned fools want to go to hell it's not our duty to stop them, if that's what they want to do.

—Attributed to Chief Justice Steon in reference to the function of the Supreme Court

° ° °

At a time when we should be sending the best we have to Great Britain, we have not done so. We have sent a rich man, untrained in diplomacy, unlearned in history and politics, who is a great publicity seeker and who is apparently amibitious to be the first Catholic president of the United States.

—Harold Ickes in a conversation with Col. Josiah Wedgwood, Liberal Member of Parliament

° ° °

Gerald Ford played football too long without a helmet.

—Johnson about Gerald Ford

° ° °

The Republicans have a "me-too" candidate running on a "yes-but" platform by a "has-been" staff.

—Stevenson about Ike Eisenhower

° ° °

Dulles is traveling so fast he seldom has the opportunity to contradict Nixon in the same country twice.

—Stevenson

° ° °

I have wondered at times what the Ten Commandments would have looked like if Moses had run it though a state legislature.

—Gov. Ronald Reagan

° ° °

Rockefeller's appetite for the Republican nomination obviously has been whetted by Romney's blundering, Nixon's wondering and Reagan's thundering.

—John Bailey, Nat'l Dem. Chairman

° ° °

The Pentagon has 5 sides on every issue.

° ° °

If a traveler were informed that such a man was leader of the House of Commons, he may begin to comprehend how the Egyptians worshipped an insect.

—Disraeli about Lord John Russell

° ° °

When you have Joe Kennedy for a friend, you don't need any enemies.

Quoted in *JFK: Man and the Myth*, Lasky

° • •

When a father was asked by his son why they had a chaplain in Congress and does he pray for the Congress, the father replied, "Oh, no, he stands up and takes a look at Congress and then prays for the country."

° • °

Mr. Nixon may be very good in kitchen debates, but so are a great many other married men I know.

—John Kennedy

• ° •

Last Thursday night Mr. Nixon dismissed me as "another Truman." I regard this as a compliment. I consider him another Dewey.

—Kennedy about Nixon

• ° •

I talked my husband into becoming a Republican in 1966. He'd always been a Democrat. And the day I talked him out of calling the President 'Tricky Dick'—I could still shoot myself!

—Martha Mitchell

• ° •

There's quite a show running in town. It's called 'How To Succeed in Washington Without Even Being There.' I'm not talking about the President. He can't leave Washington. He's much too busy greeting various members of his family as they come and go.

—Sen. Kenneth B. Keating (R-NY)

° ° °

They've been peddling eyewash about themselves and hogwash about Democrats. What they need is a good mouthwash.

—Sen. Lyndon B. Johnson

° ° °

I almost became neither a hawk nor a dove, but a chicken.

—Gov. Ronald Reagan

° ° °

If he is elected president, he'll be the first carpetbagger voter to get to the White House.

—Said about John Kennedy

° ° °

It's not Jack's money he's spending, it's yours. He may have more dollars but you have more sense.

—Nixon about Kennedy

° ° °

"That over-educated Oxford s.o.b."

—A reference to Senator William Fulbright by President Harry Truman

° ° °

Every time we have an election, we get in worse men and the country keeps right on going. Times have proven only one thing and that is you can't ruin this country even with politics.

—Will Rogers

° ° °

Politicans as a class radiate a powerful odor. Their business is almost as firmly grounded on false pretenses as that of the quack doctor or the shyster lawyer.

—H.L. Mencken

° ° °

The basic political system is like a cesspool, with hundreds of human stinkers bouncing against one another. To be in politics is to be in a toilet bowl.

° ° °

It seems to me a barren thing, this conservatism—an unhappy crossbreed, the mule of politics that engenders nothing.

—Disraeli

° ° °

Yes, I am a Jew, and when the ancestors of the right honourable gentleman were brutal savages in an unknown island, mine were priests in the Temple of Solomon.

—Disraeli's reply to a taunt by Daniel O'Connel

° ° °

When Gladstone yelled at Disraeli in the House of Commons, crying, "You, sir, will die either on the gallows or of some loathsome disease," Disraeli replied, "That sir, depends upon whether I embrace your principles or your mistress."

° ° °

DeGaulle keeps behaving like an untipped waiter.

° ° °

He may have been an affable grandfather at 70. But at 68½ he put missiles in Cuba. We don't believe anyone reforms between 68½ and 70.

—Secy. of State Rusk about Khrushchev

° ° °

"Sen. McCarthy, my gardener may call me Alice; all New

York taxi drivers may call me Alice, the policeman on my corner may call me Alice, but YOU may call me Mrs. Longworth.

—Mrs. Alice Longworth to Sen. Joe McCarthy

° ° °

Every public figure had some clay about the feet and ankles ... Not then and rarely since would I encounter a politician who was not forced to leave a part of his soul in escrow.

—Barbara Howar
Laughing All The Way

° ° °

Lenin and myself are in the same camp in one way: we believe that the main object of politics should be the abolition of the village idiot.

° ° °

Party politics is the most narrow-minded occupation in the world ... All you would have to do to make some men atheists is just to tell them the Lord belonged to the opposition political party.

—Will Rogers

° ° °

The Republicans have the ability of cutting a dollar bill in half without touching the paper.

° ° °

Well, if Gladstone fell into the Thames, that would be a misfortune; and if anybody pulled him out, that, I suppose, would be a calamity.

—Benj. Disraeli when asked to differentiate between a misfortune and a calamity

° ° °

I do not mind that Mr. Zorin called me a Western Capitalist circle, but I wonder how he would feel if I were to refer to him as a Red Square.

—Joseph Godber, British Min. at Geneva Conference

° ° °

The liberal is Mr. Janus—facing both ways. He sees two sides to every question.

—Max Lerner

° ° °

Mr. Kremelin was distinguished for his ignorance; for he had only one idea, and that was wrong.

—Benj. Disraeli

° ° °

A liberal is a man with both feet planted squarely in mid-air.

—Laski

° ° °

In Russian you say what you like about Khrushchev—but Lord help you if you say what you don't like.

° ° °

It was a consistent show of harebrained obtuseness mixed with ignorance.

—*N.Y. Times* ref. to Attorney General Saxbe

° ° °

Sen. William Fulbright ought to be crucified for his stand against Harold Carswell for appointment to the Supreme Court.

—Martha Mitchell

° ° °

Thomas E. Dewey is like the little man on the wedding cake.

—Alice Longworth

° ° °

He is a labor-baiting, poker-playing, whiskey-drinking, evil old man.

—John L. Lewis about Vice-Pres. John N. Garner

° ° °

How can you blame Rockefeller for wanting to get out of Albany? After all, Albany is where the late, late show begins at 6:30 P.M.

° ° °

There is one difference between a tax collector and a taxidermist—the taxidermist leaves the hide.

—Mortimer Caplan, Director Internal Revenue Service

° ° °

How do you expect to govern a country that has 246 kinds of cheese?

—Charles DeGaulle
Newsweek, Oct. 1, 1962

° ° °

Hypocrisy may be customary in politics but the Massachusetts Democrat seems to be making a career of it. He would rather be President than right, and in his relentless pursuit of his party's nomination, he has been trimming to every breeze.

—*Chicago Tribune Editorial* about Jack Kennedy

° ° °

It was not a large affair at all. No entertainment . . . You know when you have six or seven senators, you don't need entertainment.

—Perle Mesta about a party in honor of Mike Mansfield

° ° °

Spain has her matadors. The United States has her senators.

° ° °

Rail splitting produced an immortal President in Abraham Lincoln, but golf, with 29,000 courses, hasn't produced even a good A-Number-1 Congressman.

—Will Rogers

° ° °

When asked by the professor of his English class, "Can you give me a clear, concise definition of a politician?" the son of a congressman replied, "I can, sir, if you'll just tell me to which party you refer."

° ° °

One thing about him—he's sweet and loving—a bee flew in his mouth and he stung it. Lots of people owe a lot to him—ulcers, nausea, diarrhea.

—Said about William F. Buckley

° ° °

"How To Succeed At Harvard Without Really Trying."

—Suggested title for a campaign biography about Ted Kennedy

° ° °

Reader, suppose you were an idiot. And suppose you were a member of Congress. But I repeat myself.

—Mark Twain

° ° °

You can't use tact with a congressman. A congressman is a hog. You must take a stick and hit him on the snout.

—Henry Adams

° ° °

When one senator missed several consecutive roll calls and was reported to be in his home state mending fences, a colleague said of him: "You can't blame him for spending so much time mending that fence. That's where he's always sitting."

° ° °

"Senators, who have no secretaries of their own, may take advantage of the girls in the steno pool."

—Message to the Senate Office

° ° °

I am sick and tired of keeping my big trap shut and having everyone else leak.

—Sen. Everett Dirksen admonishment to Congress

° ° °

Death and taxes are inevitable but at least death does not become worse each time Congress meets.

—Sen. Norris Cotton (R-N.H.)

o o o

With the money I'm spending I could elect my chauffeur to Congress.

—Attributed to Joe Kennedy when his son ran for Congress

o o o

Rep. Abraham J. Multer (D-NY) claims the initials M C which follow all congressional members' names does not stand for Member of Congress but for Master of Confusion.

o o o

When it comes to its own conduct, Congress is a good deal like the infantry captain who orders his men over the top and tells them he'll be interested in the reports they bring back to him.

—Sen. Clifford P. Chase (N.J.)

o o o

Some statesmen go to Congress and some go to hell. It is the same thing, after all.

—Eugene Field

o o o

The government prints and distributes the speeches made by congressmen without the slightest profit. It might also be added they are read the same way.

o o o

During the first six months I wondered how I made it (the Senate). Later, I wondered how the rest of them made it.

—Sen. Harry Truman

o o o

There is talk of Shirley Temple in Congress. And why shouldn't she do well in politics? All her old dancing partners have.

o o o

Fleas can be taught nearly anything that a congressman can.

—Mark Twain

o o o

There are two periods when Congress does no business: one is before the holidays, and the other is after.

—G.D. Prentice

o o o

Congress: where a man gets up to speak, says nothing, and nobody listens, then everybody disagrees.

o o o

There are a lot of grindstones around here in need of noses.

—Sen. Norris Cotton

o o o

The trouble with Congress is that is doesn't stay calm and cool when collected.

o o o

I don't make jokes; I just watch the government and report the facts.

—Will Rogers

o o o

Our lawmakers in Washington think they are instruments of destiny when actually they are only wind instruments.

o o o

Sen. Kenneth B. Keating (R-NY) told about a letter from Rochester inviting him to speak. "I hope you can come, senator, because all of us would like to hear the dope from Washington."

o o o

Never put off until tomorrow what you can do today. There may be a law against it.

—Rep. Edgar Hiestand (R-Cal.)
speaking about large number of laws passed

o o o

We have the power to do any damn fool thing we want to do, and we seem to do it every ten minutes.

—Senator William Fulbright, *Time* 2/4/52

o o o

Rep. Kathryn E. Granahan (D-Pa.) reports that one morning when she hailed a cab to the House office building, the cab-driver told her, "Lady, you're an optimist if you expect to see your congressman this early in the morning.

o o o

One of the countless drawbacks of being in Congress is that I am compelled to receive impertinent letters from a jackass like you in which you say I promised to have the Sierra Madre mountains reforested and I have been in Congress two months and haven't done it. Will you please take two running jumps and go to hell.

—Rep. John Steven McGroarty (Cal.)
letter to a constituent

o o o

Bob Hope says he's glad Gerald Ford is Vice-President: "Any man who has spent 20 years in Congress deserves a rest."

° ° °

When a senator once takes the floor, nobody but Almighty God can interrupt him—and the Lord never seems to take any notice of him!

—Sen. Dem. Leader Jos. Robinson of Ark.

° ° °

When John V. Lindsay was a representative , he was awakened by his wife with the words, "John, wake up. There's a robber in the house."

"Maybe in the Senate," he grunted, "but not in the House."

° ° °

When David prepared to slay the giant, he armed himself with a handful of stones. But President Eisenhower slew the whole Republican Party in the South with one Little Rock.

—Sen. John McClellan (D-Ark)

° ° °

When I was a boy I was told that anybody could be president; I'm beginning to believe it.

—Clarence Darrow

° ° °

He strokes the ball toward the hole and yells, "Fall in!"

—Bing Crosby in regard to Eisenhower's golf

° ° °

Golf is a fine release from the tensions of office, but we get a little tired of holding the bag.

—Adlai Stevenson about Eisenhower

° ° °

I admire Gen. Eisenhower, and I like Ike; but I have some reservations regarding the President of the United States.

—Bernard Leffay—former French Minister
about Eisenhower

° ° °

It's too bad the coach and the quarterback didn't get together before they got crossed up on their signals.

—Sen. Mike Mansfield
referring to speeches by Eisenhower-Adams

° ° °

Stop blaming the President. He's not smart enough to think up all the things that have happened.

—Will Rogers,*The Man & The Times*

° ° °

The General is worried about my funnybone; I am worried about his backbone.

—Stevenson about Eisenhower

o o o

Adlai's no rail-splitter, just a hair splitter.

—Eisenhower about Stevenson

o o o

Ike is a part-time President.

—Stevenson about Eisenhower

o o o

Question: Why is the rocking chair a perfect symbol of the New Frontier? Answer: Because it provides a feeling of motion while not going anywhere.

—Republican comment about Kennedy Administration

o o o

When Kennedy was President, the widely publicized rocking chair encouraged this question: "Is the President on or off his rocker?"

o o o

In a Washington book store, G.O.P. Committee chairman Meade Alcorn noted a two volume set of the memoirs of Harry S. Truman with a sign: "originally $10—Now $1.98". "In other words," he observed, "the written word of Mr. Truman has been discounted 80%.

o o o

We used to laugh about the great risk a mosquito took in biting John Kennedy—with some of his blood the mosquito was sure to die.

—Bob Kennedy

o o o

Jack was reasonably inconspicuous.

—Prof. Ronald Ferry
said about Kennedy when a student

o o o

He'll sit here, and he'll say, "Do this! Do that!" And nothing will happen. Poor Ike—it won't be a bit like the army.

—Harry S. Truman

o o o

Jack the Knife was back from the prowl.

—Murray Kempton about Kennedy

o o o

Kennedy has made as many errors as Pope John and it will take 50 years to correct the mistakes of both.

—Senator Dodd

o o o

Mr. Speaker, you blue-bellied rascal! I have for the last thirty minutes been trying to get your attention, and each time I have caught your eye, you have wormed, twisted and squirmed like a dog with a flea in his hide, damn you!

Gentlemen, you may tear down the honored pictures from the halls of the United States Senate, desecrate the grave of George Washington, haul down the Stars and Stripes, curse the Goddess of Liberty, and knock down the tomb of U.S. Grant, but your crime would in no wise compare in enormity with what you propose to do when you would change the name of Arkansas! Change the name of Arkansas-hell-fire, no!

—Cassius M. Johnson

° ° °

America is the country where you buy a lifetime supply of aspirin for one dollar and use it up in two months.

—John Barrymore

° ° °

It's hard to believe that America was founded to get rid of taxation.

° ° °

The Republicans have their split right after election, and the Democrats have theirs just before an election.

—Will Rogers

° ° °

Asked for an example illustrating that "pro" is the opposite of "con," the student replied: "Progress and Congress."

° ° °

The bill opening the Cherokee Strip had just been passed. Congressman Heard of Missouri, who had voted for it, was leaving the Capitol, when he was met by Mrs. Hechmann who had lobbied against the measure. When she learned the bill had passed by a vote of 142 to 108, she said, "There were 142 railroad thieves, were there?"

With a bow, he nodded and said, "And only 108 cattle thieves, madam."

° ° °

Calvin Coolidge done nothin' as president, but it wasn't that he done nothin' that made him a hero—he done it better than anybody.

—Will Rogers

° ° °

It happened at the opening of the second session of the 55th Congress. Rep. Williams of Mississippi was commenting on Mr. Dingley's statement as to the picture of the government's finances, when he was asked, "Isn't the account right?"

He answered, "Yes, except in two particulars. The figures on the debit side are not right, and the figures on the credit side are all wrong."

° ° °

The congressman was trying to impress his colleagues, and as he spoke he walked up and back in front of them. Came a shout from one of them:

If you're talkin' stop walkin!
If you're walkin' stop talkin!

° ° °

"Is there a criminal lawyer in Congress?"

"We think so, but we haven't been able to prove it to him."

° ° °

The newly installed senator died quite suddenly. His Negro valet remarked, "He didn't have no doctah, he died a natural death."

° ° °

About Congress:"That may be so, I do not know;
It sounds so awful queer.
I don't dispute your word at all
But don't spread that bull in here."

° ° °

George Washington was once at a dinner party, where his host had set him with his back to a red-hot stove. After some squirming, he beat a retreat for a more comfortable position, at the same time explaining the reason, "Why," said the hostess, "I thought an old general like you could stand fire better than that." "I never could stand fire in my rear," replied the general.

° ° °

He fiddled while Detroit burned. He faddled while men died.

—Barry Goldwater attacking Pres. Johnson

° ° °

Republicans told the story during Kennedy's administration. There were two birds sitting on a branch of a tree talking about Pres. Kennedy. "I like JFK," said the first bird. "Why?" asked the second. "Because he's for us," replied the first.

° ° °

The presidency is not a good place to make new friends. I'm going to keep my old friends.

—John Kennedy

° ° °

Maybe the country would have been better off if I had been a concert pianist.

—Former Pres. Harry S. Truman

° ° °

Al Capp (creator of Li'l Abner) was hustled by a Washington hostess during a cocktail party to meet an important guest. She said to the guest, "Mr. Truman, I'd like you to meet the famous comic strip cartoonist, Al Capp." Truman asked "Which comic strip?" She then turned to Capp and said, "I'd like to introduce you to President Truman." Capp asked, "Which country?"

° ° °

If I were in the White House I would not be sitting around or playing golf; I'd be doing something about the recession.

—Harry S. Truman
about Eisenhower

° ° °

Businessmen in Washington are ordering a new drink which they call a Kennedy Cocktail—stocks on the rocks.

—Told during Kennedy administration

° ° °

A sound government to the Republicans is the kind of government where the President makes nice sounds, while the Vice-President snarls.

—Harry Truman
about the Republican Administration

° ° °

Pres. Nixon silenced a heckler with: "The jawbone of an ass is just as dangerous a weapon today as it was in Samson's time."

° ° °

PEOPLE, PLACES AND THINGS
Introduction

"People, Places and Things" makes up the final section of this cynical, witty, uncensored book of affronts, insults and indignities.

Why this title for this chapter? If this were the opening section, it could be considered as an introduction of sorts, a varied sampling somewhat like the reception tendered prior to a banquet, where offerings of fish, fowl, fruit, and meats are arrayed on long tables. Though a steak dinner will be served later, men and women rush about in haste, flitting from serving dish to serving dish, dipping here, nibbling there, tasting this and that. They eat as though there will be no tomorrow. They are not worried that a full belly makes a dull brain. Of course some of the guests later on remember well the words of C.T. Copeland, "To eat is human; to digest, divine."

But, "People, Places and Things" is a final chapter and so might better be compared to mom's favorite kitchen concoction. Believe me, seasoned to taste, it is usually delicious! After all, it is made up of all sorts of delicacies left over from previous meals. But what is the concoction?—hash or smorgasbord?

My own feeling is, who cares! Take your pick! I have tried to fill this chapter with refreshing bits of humor and irony. True, each of the selections might have been appropriately placed in one of the previous sections—affronts about marriage, in the section on Family Living; indignities heaped on government officials in the section called The Political Arena. My own aim was to surprise the reader by offering in one chapter a variety of insults, not like the main dish at a banquet, but rather like the culinary delicacies at the reception. I aimed for a laugh, a chuckle, a bundle of surprises. This required that I take into account the many oddities of people—their likes, dislikes, hangups, their institutions and their places.

To the best of my knowledge, no quote in this section is anemic. They pack their own punch, and are based on the assumption that no matter what you are trying to communicate, one good snappy line is worth a thousand words. In today's age of incredible swift communication and "time is of the essence" philosophy, a succinct phrase, a quick comeback is urgent.

A good deal of this chapter will bring sparkle to your conversation, brilliance to your writings, and zing to your repartee. Discretion should be applied, however, in the use of insults. They are sharp tools, not to be toyed with. Always use your brains. Think before you speak. And when you speak say something. Do not say all that you know, but always know what you say. Don't bore. Remember a bore is one who is interesting to a point—the point of departure.

Go ahead now and taste, and having tasted, hold on to what is good. My own conclusion might be helpful to you as well. So,

I sit beside my lonely fire
And pray for wisdom yet:
The insults to remember
The booing to forget.

PEOPLE, PLACES AND THINGS

The worst winter I ever spent was one summer in San Francisco.

—Mark Twain

o o o

Every Irishman has a potato in his head.

—J.C. & A.W. Hare

o o o

An Irishman's heart is nothing but his imagination.

—Bernard Shaw

o o o

Irish men have hardly enough sex to perpetuate their own cantankerous species.

—Arland Usher, Historian

o o o

The common Englishman is prone to forget a cardinal article in the bill of social rights, that every man has a right to his own ears.

—Emerson

o o o

No pig-eyed bag of wind is going to push us out of Berlin.

—Frank L. Howley about Khrushchev's threats

o o o

The Communists offer a Utopian vision which is not particularly attractive to two types: the ignorant and the degenerate.

o o o

Russia's ability to send a man to Mars would be a big step toward world peace—if she sent the right man.

° ° °

The British are fond of sports. One of their favorite amusements is running themselves down.

—Lord Chandes

° ° °

"You are a Jew, are you not?" demanded the bigoted and prejudiced Yankee to the small man he found seated next to him on the train.

"Yes, I am a Jew," admitted the man.

"Well, I'm not," said the Yankee proudly, "and I am happy to say that in the village I come from there is not a single Jew."

"That's why it's still a village," said the Jew.

° ° °

America was better off when we had more whittlers and a fewer number of chiselers.

° ° °

If there ever was an aviary overstocked with jays, it is that Yaptown-on-the-Hudson called New York.

—O'Henry

° ° °

French coffee is made by running a chicory bean against a coffee bean and dropping the chicory bean in the water.

—Mark Twain, about the poor quality of French coffee

° ° °

"Take this mess away," said John Randolph, the American statesman, handing the waiter his cup and saucer, "change it."

"Do you want coffee or tea?" asked the confused waiter.

"If that is tea, bring me coffee. If it is coffee, bring me tea. I want a change."

° ° °

"Why is it," asked a Frenchman of a Swiss, "that you Swiss always fight for money, while we French only fight for honor?"

"I suppose," said the Swiss, "that each fight for what they lack."

° ° °

Now when they (Congress) get the Constitution all fixed up they are going to start in on the Ten Commandments, just as soon as they can find somebody in Washington who has read them.

—Will Rogers

° ° °

We are here for a spell and pass on. Any man that thinks

civilization has advanced is an egotist . . . We know a lot of things we used to dident know, but we dont know any way to prevent 'em happening.

Ibid

o o o

If we can just improve their (women's) marksmanship, we can improve civilization. About every fourth fellow you meet nowadays ought to be shot.

Ibid

o o o

He is the kind of gossip who is always caught in his mouth trap.

o o o

Some carve their way to the top; he chisels.

o o o

Babies haven't any hair; old men's heads are just as bare;
Between the cradle and the grave lie just a haricut and a shave.

o o o

A wig makes it possible for my wife to put a new top on an old chassis.

o o o

He was lovesick and took the first pill that came along.

o o o

A scandal is a breeze stirred up by a couple of windbags.

o o o

Some people are asked for autographs—he, for his fingerprints.

o o o

Some speakers drive home facts; he drives the audience.

o o o

Looking at modern art is like trying to follow the plot in a bowl of alphabet soup.

o o o

Nothing makes it easier for a psychiatrist to sleep than having patients.

o o o

If he were just a little more narrow-minded, his ear would be on the wrong side of his head.

o o o

"If you really loved me," said the wife, "you would have married some other woman."

o o o

There are two periods in life when a man doesn't understand

a woman—before marriage and after marriage.

° ° °

"I'll have you know that I'm nobody's fool!"

"Cheer up, boy. Maybe somebody will adopt you."

° ° °

It's funny how we never get too old to learn some new way to be stupid.

° ° °

There are more bankers in Ossining, N.Y. than any town its size in the United States.

—Will Rogers

° ° °

The congressmen and senators are not supposed to know anything about the country, and they generally don't, so the president issues his message.

Ibid

° ° °

She thought she bought a dress for a ridiculous price, when in reality she bought it for an absurd figure.

° ° °

What a switch! His teeth are real, but his tongue is false!

° ° °

If Adam came back to earth, the only thing he would recognize would be the jokes.

° ° °

It's dangerous to drive in a fog especially if it's mental.

° ° °

It was a wise man who remarked that he who carries tale makes monkey of self.

° ° °

You can send a message around the world in a seventh of a second, yet it may take years to force a simple idea through one-quarter inch of human skull.

° ° °

"I'll have the suit ready for you in 30 days," said the tailor.

"Thirty days!" protested the customer. "Why, God created the entire world in six days."

"True enough," said the tailor. "And take a good look at it now!"

° ° °

The man who says, "I run things at my house," usually refers to the lawn mower, the washing machine, the dryer, the vacuum cleaner, and the errands."

° ° °

She's a shrinking violet who minds her own business at the top of her voice.

° ° °

"My grandfather," boasted a boor, "fought in the Zula War."
"You don't say," came back the answer, "On which side?"

° ° °

"What were your father's last words before he died?"
"He didn't have any. Mama was with him to the very end."

° ° °

A brassiere is an invention designed to make a mountain out of a molehill, and vice versa.

° ° °

Monologue—one woman talking.
Catalogue—two women talking.

° ° °

He has the art of using meaningless words to say a lot of nothing.

° ° °

A woman went to the meat market the other day and ordered a dollar's worth of steak. The butcher replied, "Sister, you just said a mouthful!"

° ° °

While America has turned out some great men, there are quite a few others not so great that it should turn out.

° ° °

Most of the stumbling blocks he complains about is right under his own hat.

° ° °

To argue with a woman is like going into a shower bath with an umbrella over you. What good does it do?

° ° °

When Columbus started out, he didn't know where he was going. When he got there, he didn't know where he was. When he got back, he didn't know where he had been. And he did it all on other people's money. What a politician Columbus would have been today!

° ° °

This sign was noted at the National Zoological Garden in Washington: LOST CHILDREN WILL BE TAKEN TO THE LION HOUSE.

° ° °

News Item: The fire was put out before the fire department could do much damage.

° ° °

A small boy and a fat man were riding side by side on a crowded bus. Two women were standing in front of them. Said the fat man, "Why don't you get up and give one of these ladies your seat?"

Replied the small boy: "Why don't you get up and let them both sit down?"

o o o

A statesman is made of the right kind of timber when he can lead the people out of the woods.

o o o

Knocking is caused by two things—carbon and envy.

o o o

It took Confucius to observe: "Man who cover chair instead of territory is on bottom all time."

o o o

The average American takes 19,689 steps daily—mostly in the wrong direction.

o o o

Television is a device that permits people who haven't anything to do to watch people who can't do anything.

—*Washington Times-Herald*

o o o

They're an ideal couple; they think alike about everything but she always thinks first.

o o o

Look at him and you'll see that many square meals made him round.

o o o

An editor retracted: "We hereby apologize for our esteemed citizen, Henry Jones, who recently attended the horse show and, mistaken for a horse, was given a blue ribbon. It was not the horse show; it was the dog show."

o o o

"Lot's wife looked back and turned into a pillar of salt; my mother looked back once when she was driving and turned into a telephone pole."

o o o

"I just got out of prison this morning," a traveler told a man on the train. "It's going to be tough, facing old friends."

"I can sympathize with you," replied the other; "I'm just getting home from Congress."

o o o

The best way to save face is to keep the lower end of it shut.

° ° °

He puts up a big bluff and always stumbles over it.

° ° °

Wonder why they put so many holes in Swiss cheese when it's Limburger that really needs ventilation.

° ° °

Take the conceit out of some men, and they would be like a ribless umbrella.

° ° °

The average girl would rather have beauty than brains, because she knows the average man can see better than he can think.

° ° °

Many of the so-called marriage failures are caused by failures marrying.

° ° °

If people learn through their mistakes we know a few fellows who seem to be getting a fantastic education.

° ° °

It's too bad that he has such a bright future behind him.

° ° °

Diplomacy is the ability to take something and act as if you were giving it away.

° ° °

Some men blaze a way; others only blaze away.

° ° °

The first signs of spring are the blooming idiots on the highway.

° ° °

Never argue with a fool. Onlookers may not be able to tell who is which.

° ° °

Sometimes a speech is like a wheel—the longer the spoke, the greater the tire.

° ° °

"Do you want a large or small picture?" asked the photographer.

"Just a small one," replied the talkative client.

"Then close your mouth!"

° ° °

A haircut can do a great deal to change your appearance. Grandma got one of those mod haircuts. Now she doesn't look like an old lady any more. She looks like an old man.

° ° °

There's no fool like an old fool. You just can't beat experience.

° ° °

I wish his halo would fall just a few inches so that it can become a noose around his neck.

° ° °

A girdle is a device used to keep an unfortunate condition from spreading.

° ° °

Certainly you can't fool all of the people all of the time. Quite a few of them are busy fooling you.

° ° °

Many ideas, like many people, look good until you try them out.

° ° °

The bigger his head, the easier it is to fill his shoes.

° ° °

There is just as much horse sense as ever, but it seems like the horses have it.

° ° °

He spends half his time wishing for things he could have if he didn't spend half his time wishing.

° ° °

Nature left a hole in his mind, which he plastered over with a thick coat of conceit.

° ° °

Some cars have fluid drive, but with him, he's just a drip at the wheel.

° ° °

A duck is a bird that walks as though it had been riding a horse all day.

° ° °

With the rashness of ignorance the uninitiated dare to dabble in affairs of state.

—John of Salisbury

° ° °

This struggle and scramble for office, for a way to live without work, will finally test the strength of our institutions.

—Abraham Lincoln

° ° °

Imagination was given a man to compensate him for what he is not, and a sense of humor was provided to console him for what he is.

° ° °

Some people are like coffee—98 percent of the active ingredients have been removed from the bean.

o o o

An inventor claims to have produced a mechanical man that can talk without thinking. That's nothing new. We've heard lots of them.

o o o

The price of hogs has been steadily advancing but the road hogs are as cheap as ever.

o o o

The ears and throat are sympathetically connected, we are told. That is probably the reason why so many things we hear give us a pain in the neck.

o o o

He can stay longer in an hour than most people can in a week.

o o o

He would be brilliant if he retained as much of what he read as of what he eats.

o o o

Some self-made men must have bribed the building inspector.

o o o

An optimist is a guy who talks about how big a fool he used to be.

o o o

A closed mind, like a closed room, can become awfully stuffy.

o o o

A philosopher likened marriage to a violin: After the beautiful music is over, the strings are still attached.

o o o

The good die young. You will probably live on to a ripe old age.

o o o

He talks so quickly that he says things he hasn't even thought of.

o o o

"To me," said the newlywed, "romance was like a game of chess. I made one false move and found I was mated."

o o o

"Did you wake up grumpy this morning?" asked the marriage counselor of his female client.

"No," was the immediate reply. "I just let him sleep."

o o o

If he can remember so many jokes,
With all the details that mold them,
Why can't he recall, with equal skill,
All the times he's told them!

o o o

Nobody gives a groom a shower because he's all washed up already.

o o o

A few students do have the spark of genius, but he seems to have ignition trouble.

o o o

He claims he never made a mistake and so surely must be tired of doing nothing.

o o o

"Three of those apples I bought this morning were rotten," she complained bitterly.

"That's all right, Madam. You need not bring them back. Your word is just as good as the apples."

o o o

Humorists are not the only ones who make up jokes. Look what the beauticians sometimes turn out.

o o o

With his long face, he can't be very broad-minded.

o o o

A great many so-called open minds should be closed for repairs.

o o o

Insults Taken from Examination Papers:

Capital punishment in the state of Ohio is death by elocution.

All brutes are imperfect animals. Man alone is the perfect beast.

Ramsay MacDonald was the prime mixture in England.

The population of London is a bit too dense.

o o o

Most people can play at least one musical instrument; usually a horn.

o o o

He sent in his poem with the notation: "Let me know at once whether you can use it as I have other irons in the fire."

The editor replied: "Remove irons; insert poem."

o o o

She called her husband *Theory* because he never worked out.

° ° °

There is an off season for nearly all flowers except blooming idiots.

° ° °

Nature was kind to construct a man in such a way so that he cannot kick himself.

° ° °

He means well but his meanness is greater than his wellness.

° ° °

He is like a whale—since he got to the top he blows.

° ° °

Historians tell us that women in the Middle Ages used cosmetics. For that matter, women in the Middle Ages, and even after that, still use them.

° ° °

Too often a crossing is the meeting place of light heads and headlights.

° ° °

If you marry a grocer, you get groceries for nothing; if you marry a doctor, you get well for nothing; if you marry a preacher, you get good for nothing.

° ° °

This country would not be in such a mess if the Indians had adopted more stringent immigration laws.

° ° °

An actress congratulated Ilka Chase on her book, *Past Imperfect*. "I enjoyed it," she said. "Who wrote it for you?"

"Darling," clawed back Ilka, "I'm so delighted you like it. Who read it to you?"

° ° °

I don't go so far as to think that the only good Indians are the dead Indians, but I believe nine out of every ten are, and I shouldn't like to inquire too closely into the case of the tenth. The most vicious cowboy has less moral principle than the average Indian.

—Theodore Roosevelt

° ° °

The closest thing to immortality in America is a government bureau.

° ° °

It ain't so much the things that people don't know that makes trouble in this world, as it is the things that people know that ain't so.

—Mark Twain

° ° °

In the great American bedlam we just move from bunk to bunk.

° ° °

It is with narrow-minded people as with narrow-necked bottles: the less they have in them the more noise they make pouring it out.

—Alexander Pope

° ° °

The fanciest wardrobes belong to dummies.

° ° °

Since ants and horseflies are not likely to discover the formula for the atomic bomb, they are likely to outlive man by as long a time as they preceded him.

—Kaplan

° ° °

Fuehrers and dictators are human bellwethers. They lead their followers both to the pasture and to the slaughterhouse.

° ° °

Policy without power is as effective as Security Council resolutions.

° ° °

George Bernard Shaw brings down the tragic to the trivial. Kafka generally raises the trivial to the tragic.

—Kaplan

° ° °

A rich fool is like a poor oil painting richly framed.

° ° °

There is an old story about a donkey being disguised with a lion's skin. Every now and then some college does the same thing with a sheepskin.

° ° °

How does it happen that so many wise guys are working for so many dumb heads?

° ° °

If you cannot believe anything you hear and only half of what you see, better be careful of what you think.

° ° °

She has such a turned-up nose that when she sneezes she blows off her hat.

° ° °

A folk singer is a fellow who sings through his nose by ear.

° ° °

He couldn't live happily ever after because he was after too much.

° ° °

This is the tragedy of his life
This sums up his fate;
He is getting old too soon
And getting wise too late.

° ° °

If he would only lose his reputation he would be lucky.

° ° °

If some politicians would walk straight, they'd run better.

° ° °

The wealth he needs isn't as much dollars as it is sense.

° ° °

When he says he is going out of his mind, he isn't taking a long trip at all.

° ° °

Wind up a gossip and she runs somebody down.

° ° °

People and boats each toot the loudest when they're in a fog.

° ° °

Did you hear about that girl hippy who was getting married? Instead of giving her a shower, they made her take one.

° ° °

Politics is like apple pie—crust and a lot of applesauce.

° ° °

We teach the children Danish, trigonometry, and Spanish; fill their heads with modern notions, and the secrets of the oceans, and the hieroglyph inscriptions from the land of the Egyptians; learn the date of every battle, know the habits of the cattle, know the time of every crowning, read the poetry of Browning; make them show a preference for each musty branch of science; tell the acreage of Sweden, and the serpent's wiles in Eden; and the other things we teach'em make a mountain so immense that we have not a moment left to teach them common sense!

—*Sunshine Magazine*

° ° °

He is like a tack and can go only as far as his head will let him.

° ° °

In some beauty salons the talk alone can curl your hair.

° ° °

Some folks lie in wait; others lie in weight.

° ° °

The idea of a man picking a wife is about as absurd as that of an apple picking a farmer.

° ° °

He proposed on his knees with a speech tender-sweet,
And it took him ten years to get back on his feet.

° ° °

A class reunion is where you get together to see who is falling apart.

° ° °

Every time the professor erases the blackboard he demonstrates what he has in mind.

° ° °

Elsewhere it might be a dish of pretzels, a plate of salad, a bird's nest, or a coal scuttle, but if you see it sitting on top of a woman's head, it is a hat.

° ° °

Dear Sir,

I being a gentleman cannot dictate what I think of you. My secretary being a lady cannot type it. You being neither will understand exactly what I mean.

—L. Lawrence

° ° °

Many wise words are spoken in jest, but they don't compare with the number of foolish words spoken in earnest.

° ° °

It seems that about all some people have learned during the last decade is how to go faster, work less, spend more money, and die quicker.

° ° °

My neighbor is a real bore—here today and here tomorrow. He throws his mouth into high gear before his brain turns over. He could reach a greater height if he had a little more depth. He thinks he has an open mind when the truth is it's only vacant. He goes through life looking for something soft when all the time it is under his hat. He so wants to have his own way, he writes his diary a week ahead of time.

° ° °

A Texan arrived at the gate of his eternal abode and remarked: "I never thought heaven could be so much like Texas."

"Son," replied the gatekeeper, "You're not in heaven."

° ° °

Postal clerk, to woman mailing the old family Bible to her brother in a distant city: "Does this package contain anything breakable?"

"Just the Ten Commandments," was the answer.

° ° °

Many people have the philisophy of: Sin Now—Pay Later.

° ° °

Customer in drugstore on a Sunday morning: "Please give me change of a dime."

Druggist: "Here it is. I hope you'll enjoy the sermon."

° ° °

St. Peter: "Where are you from, son?"

Man: "I'm from Texas, where else!"

St. Peter: "Well, come on in; but you aren't going to like it."

° ° °

Right now would really be an awful time for the meek to inherit the earth.

° ° °

Looking over the rim of the volcano's crater, the American tourist remarked: "Reminds one of hell, doesn't it?"

The guide shrugged his shoulders and exclaimed: "These Americans. They've been everywhere."

° ° °

If you can't stand solitude, maybe you bore others too.

° ° °

It generally takes twice as long to tell what he thinks than what he knows.

° ° °

Naturalists who claim America's wild life is disappearing don't stay up very late at night.

° ° °

"How is your wife getting along with her reducing diet?"

"Just excellent. She disappeared completely last week."

° ° °

A pessimist is a man who looks at the world through morose colored glasses.

° ° °

He carries his own stumbling block around with him but he camouflages it with a hat.

° ° °

The head of a soap company received the following letter from one of its customers: "Gentlemen, your soap is great! My mother-in-law fell on a cake and busted her jaw."

° ° °

Most folks have presence of mind. The trouble is absence of thought.

o o o

He imagines he has a natural bent, when he is just too lazy to straighten up.

o o o

Push-buttons have taken the place of all kinds of cranks except human ones.

o o o

Those who go to college and never get out are called professors.

• o •

If you want to see a football game in the worst way, take your wife along.

o o o

A running mate is a husband who dared talk back.

o o o

He reveals his ignorance all the time by telling people how much he knows.

o o o

Indians used to scalp their enemies . . . Nowadays government officials do the skinning.

o o o

Half the world is composed of people who have something to say and don't, and the other half who have nothing to say and keep saying it.

—Frost

o o o

Some people are so narrow-minded they can look through a keyhole with both eyes at the same time.

o o o

He doesn't have an open mind; it is just too porous to hold a conviction.

o o o

Minds, like streams, may be so broad that they are shallow.

o o o

How can he make a deep impression when he is such a shallow thinker!

o o o

The most annoying thing about a stand-patter, is not his stand, but his patter.

o o o

He works eight hours and sleeps eight hours. The trouble is it is the same eight hours.

° ° °

Young lady to young man: "If our romance were on television, I'd switch channels."

° ° °

The reason ideas die quickly in some heads is because they can't stand solitary confinement.

° ° °

He tells little white lies but they pick up dirt on the way.

° ° °

Speaking of unemployment—the human brain has more than ten billion cells.

° ° °

Some people use language to express thought, some to conceal thought; he uses it instead of thought.

° ° °

She's too young for Medicare and too old for me to care.

° ° °

Politicians are like old shirts; they only come clean in hot water.

° ° °

He's like a blister; he doesn't show up till the work is done.

° ° °

If he said what he thinks, he'd be speechless.

° ° °

Leisure time is when your wife can't find you.

° ° °

Money may talk, but today's dollar doesn't have cents enough to say very much.

° ° °

Wife to husband: "If you're looking for the fish you caught, I froze it in an ice cube."

° ° °

"Did you know," asked the guide, "that it took millions and millions of years to make the Grand Canyon?"

"Well, well," answered the tourist. "I didn't know this was a government job."

° ° °

Little drops of water, little grains of sand, make the mighty ocean and the ditto land.

But why these drops of water and little grains of sand are always served with spinach we do not understand.

° ° °

These new weather satellites are great scientific achievements. It now takes the weather bureau only half the usual time to give the wrong forecast.

o o o

The French are miserable and inhibited in their lovemaking.

—*La Realite Sexuelle*

o o o

General Sherman is often credited with saying that if he owned both hell and Texas, he would rent out Texas and live in the other place.

"That's right, every man for his own country," a Texan replied.

o o o

A German and a Russian were fishing on the opposite sides of the river that divided the Russian and American zones. The German caught fish after fish, while the Russian didn't get a bite. Finally, the Russian yelled across the river, "How is it you catch fish and I get none?"

The German thought a minute, then replied, "I guess on your side they're afraid to open their mouths."

o o o

Democracy is also a form of religion; it is the worship of jackals by jackasses.

—H.L. Mencken

o o o

America is one long expectoration.

—Oscar Wilde

o o o

Frenchmen resemble apes, who, climbing up a tree from branch to branch, never cease going till they come to the highest branch, and there show their bare behinds.

—Montaigne in his *Essays*

o o o

They dress alike, they talk alike, they think alike. What sheep!

—Lord Northcliffe about Americans

o o o

They are a race of convicts, and ought to be thankful for anything we allow them short of hanging.

—Samuel Johnson of Americans

o o o

Depressions may bring people closer to the church—but so do funerals.

—Clarence Darrow

o o o

When Churchill was hit with a large cabbage while making a speech, he said, "I asked for the gentleman's ears—not his head."

° ° °

Russia is a place where you are allowed to go anywhere they please.

° ° °

He is suffering from bottle fatigue.

° ° °

They are putting things on the screen now—you wouldn't even find on a French postcard.

° ° °

We stay awake watching movies on T.V. which put us to sleep when we saw them in the local movies years ago.

° ° °

The Eiffel Tower looks like an erector set that made good.

° ° °

Britain today is suffering from galloping obsolescence.

—British M.P. Anthony Wedgwood Bonn

° ° °

A smug Englishman once declined a cigar from Pope Pius IX with the comment, "Thank you, Your Holiness, but I am not addicted to this vice." The cigar-smoking Pontiff snapped back, "It isn't a vice or you would be addicted."

° ° °

Queen Elizabeth I of England was known as the Virgin Queen and those who have seen pictures of her with her long nose and red wig can understand why.

° ° °

Dealing with Russia is like handling an ornery jackass. You can talk to him and talk to him, but watch out he don't kick you. That's what we've got; we're dealing with a jackass.

—Senator Alexander Wiley

° ° °

If Communism is as wonderful as they claim it is, it looks like they would take down their iron curtain and put in some windows.

° ° °

When the Hun is poor and down
He's the humblest man in town;
But once he climbs and holds the rod
He smites his fellow-man and God.

—Joseph Cats

° ° °

You should study the Peerage . . . It is the best fiction that the English have ever done.

—Oscar Wilde

° ° °

Golda Meir, Israel's Prime Minister, to her visitors who begin their comments with deprecatory observations: "Don't be so humble—you're not that great."

° ° °

Only Americans think America is important; no one else does.

—Brendan Behan

° ° °

Speaking through the voice of an interpreter is like kissing a girl through the intermediary of a postman.

—Nikita Khrushchev

° ° °

Put three Zionists in a room—and they will form four political parties.

—Levi Eshkol, Hon. Prime Minister of Israel

° ° °

Too much of the world is run on the theory that you don't need road manners if you are a five-ton truck.

— *El Paso Herald*

° ° °

The Bell System is like a big dragon. You kick it in the tail, and two years later, it feels it in its head.

—Frederick Kappel

° ° °

Boston is a moral and intellectual nursery always busy applying first principles to trifles.

—George Santayana in *The Later Years*

° ° °

In a small town the jury convened the inquiry into a case of suicide. After sitting through the evidence, the twelve men retired, and after deliberating, returned the following verdict: "The jury are all of one mind—temporarily insane."

° ° °

We don't bother much about dress and manners in England, because, as a nation we don't dress well and we've no manners.

—George Bernard Shaw

° ° °

I was born in England, I will fight for England and die in England. But I'm damned if I'll live in England.

—Sir Cedric Hardwicke

o o o

The proud German Army has once again proved the truth of the saying, "The Hun is always either at your throat or at your feet."

—Sir Winston Churchill, speech May 19, 1943

o o o

The King blew his nose twice, and wiped the royal perspiration repeatedly from a face which is probably the largest uncivilized spot in England.

—O.W. Holmes about William IV

o o o

No Englishman has any common sense, or ever had, or ever will have.

—George Bernard Shaw

o o o

For Allah created the English mad—the maddest of all mankind.

—Rudyard Kipling

o o o

The whole strength of England lies in the fact that the enormous majority of the English people are snobs.

—George Bernard Shaw

o o o

A camel is what a horse would look like if it were put together by a committee.

o o o

He doesn't own a barber shop. At his prices, it's a clip joint.

o o o

There isn't much to see in a small town, but what you hear makes up for it.

o o o

Suburbia is where the builder bulldozes down the trees, then names the streets after them.

—Bill Vaughan

o o o

And this is good old Boston,
The home of the bean and the cod,
Where the Lowells talk to the Cabots,
And the Cabots talk only to God.

—John Collins Bossidy

o o o

I say it's spinach, and I say the hell with it.

—E.B. White